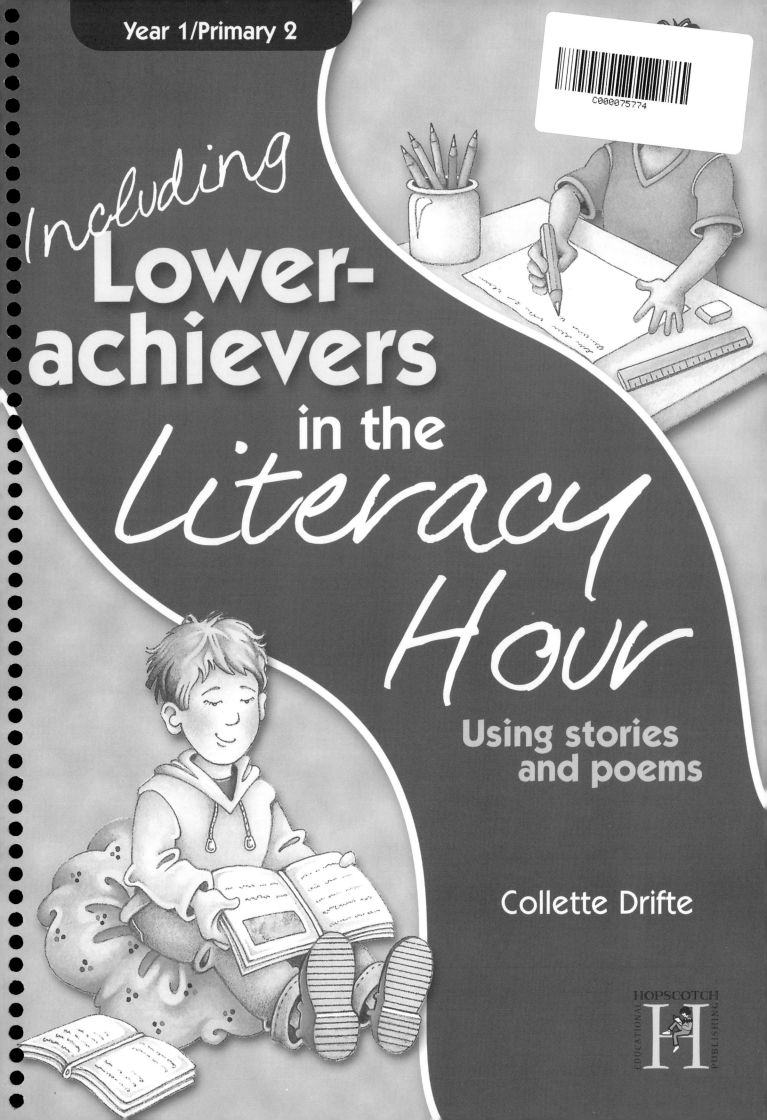

Year 1/Primary 2

Including
Lower-achievers
in the
Literacy Hour

Using stories and poems

Collette Drifte

HOPSCOTCH
EDUCATIONAL PUBLISHING

Contents

Published by
Hopscotch Educational Publishing Ltd,
29 Waterloo Place,
Leamington Spa CV32 5LA
Tel: 01926 744227

© 2001 Hopscotch Educational Publishing

Written by Collette Drifte
Series design by Blade Communications
Illustrated by Susan Hutchison
Printed by Clintplan, Southam

ISBN 1-902239-61-X

Collette Drifte hereby asserts her moral right to
be identified as the author of this work in
accordance with the Copyright, Designs and
Patents Act, 1988.

About the series

Including Lower-achievers in the Literacy Hour is a series of books aimed at enabling all children, regardless of ability, to access the learning requirements set out in the *National Literacy Strategy Framework for Teaching*. There are six books in the series, one for each of the Primary Years 1–6 (Scottish Primary 2-7). They are designed to be used by teachers or other adults working with lower-achievers in the mainstream classroom.

The books offer a structured approach which provides detailed lesson plans to teach specific skills and goals as outlined in the *National Literacy Strategy Framework for Teaching*. The lesson plans cover work at text, sentence and word levels and target a learning objective from each term's work.

Since lower-achievers often learn at a slower rate than other children, and therefore would have some difficulty in covering the whole year's work within that time, the areas and skills which cause the most problems for these children have been addressed. For example, concepts such as sequencing or predicting are included.

A feature of the series is the provision of several resource and generic sheets for each lesson, which are aimed at considerably reducing teacher preparation time. Permission is granted by the author and publisher to photocopy these sheets for educational purposes within the school or organisation that has purchased this book. The sheets are designed to reinforce the teaching point and offer the child an opportunity to practise the skill being taught. The lesson plans also offer several activities to further consolidate the point. These are designed to be done either with an adult providing close support or with a degree of independence.

The generic sheets can be used with the lesson plans as explained or used by the teacher in a different way according to the needs of the children.

On page 5 is a list of assessment focuses which can be used as an individual assessment record for the children. This page is also photocopiable.

About this book

This book is for teachers of children in Year 1 (Scottish Primary 2). It aims to:

- enable lower-achievers to be introduced to and enjoy a wide range of stories and poems;
- focus on concepts that are essential for the wider development of the literacy skills of lower-achievers;
- encourage lower-achievers to tackle challenging and diverse tasks;
- enable lower-achievers to access aspects of the *National Literacy Strategy Framework for Teaching.*

The book should be seen, however, as part of a wider strategy by the teacher to address the difficulties of lower-achievers. Such children need a great deal of repetition, practice and consolidation. Therefore, the teacher needs to utilise as many resources as possible to ensure a varied approach which offers these.

The professional audience using this book covers a vast range, from the Newly Qualified Teacher facing their first class, to the 'old hands' who have many years' experience behind them and from the teacher who has never worked with lower-achievers before, to the Classroom Assistant who has worked with such children for a long time. Therefore, any scripting or suggestions regarding the delivery of a teaching point can be easily adapted (or even disregarded!) to suit the individual needs of the professional and/or children in question. The whole essence of teaching lower-achievers is to offer individualism and flexibility.

Chapter content

There are three suggested lesson plans in the 'story' chapters and two in the 'poetry' chapters.

Overall aims

These outline the aims for the lessons set out in each chapter.

Featured book/poems

For stories, this section names the book being used, the author and a brief synopsis of the story.

In the case of a poetry chapter, it lists the poems being used, the poet and the page number where there is a photocopiable version of the poems. This can be enlarged for shared reading in the whole-class session.

A feature of all the lesson plans is that the teaching points can be repeated using other texts or poems of the teacher's choice. This is useful if the chosen text is not favoured by the teacher, or if they need to provide more repetition and consolidation of a teaching point.

Intended learning

This sets out the specific aims for each individual lesson within the chapter.

With the whole class

This outlines a whole-class introduction to the lesson. Because the class is together at this point, the lower-achievers will have the support of their peers and also the opportunity to follow the answers to any questions raised by the other children.

With the lower-achievers

This is the main body of the lesson, since it is designed to be done with the lower-achieving group. The adult-led activities are designed to be done together with an adult closely supporting. The activities are designed to utilise an adult, not necessarily the teacher. The independent activities are designed for the lower-achievers to do without as much close support and supervision. However, the term 'independent' does not imply that the child should be left totally unaided or unsupervised. This is something to be decided at the discretion of the adult/teacher, who will know how much the child is capable of doing without support. A lower-achiever may need help at any point in a lesson and should always have access to an adult to provide that help and support.

The activities suggested may be adjusted to suit the needs of the children. They are intended to offer a variety of ways of tackling the same teaching point and are not necessarily a list to be worked through. To cover all the problems of the children would be impossible, so professional judgement has to be used. For example, occasionally cutting and sticking is required, which may be difficult for the child who has problems with motor control – here the adult can assist; some of the activities require writing, so judgement must be used whether the child needs a scribe.

Plenary session

This offers suggestions for what to do with the whole class at the end of the lesson in order to summarise and explore the learning undertaken in the lesson. This should not just be a 'show and tell' session but rather an opportunity for the children to demonstrate their learning. The lower-achievers should be encouraged to play a part in the session.

Acknowledgements

Stories

Poor Monty, Anne Fine, Mammoth 1996; *Funnybones*, Allan & Janet Ahlberg, Puffin (a publishing division of Penguin Books Ltd) 1999; *Terrible Tuesday*, Hazel Townson & Tony Ross, Andersen Press 1985; *Burglar Bill*, Allan & Janet Ahlberg, Puffin (a publishing division of Penguin Books Ltd) 1999; *Backseat's Special Day*, Scoular Anderson, Hippo/Scholastic Ltd 1996; *Whiff or How the Beautiful Big Fat Smelly Baby Found a Friend*, Ian Whybrow & Russell Ayto, Doubleday Books 1999; *Titch*, Pat Hutchins, Red Fox 1997; *Where the Wild Things Are*, Maurice Sendak, HarperCollins 1992

Poems

'If' by Christopher Rowe; 'Sing a song of work to do' by Christopher Rowe and Barbara Ireson; 'If I were a king' by Barbara Ireson; 'If you should meet a giant' by Barbara Ireson; all from *Over and Over Again* by Christopher Rowe and Barbara Ireson, Beaver Books, 1978, reproduced by kind permission of the authors.

'Pick 'n' Mix Zoo' by Celia Warren from *First Verses* by John Foster and Carol Thompson, Oxford University Press 1996, reproduced by permission of the author.

'Three purple elephants' by Joan Poulson from *Action Rhymes* by John Foster, Oxford University Press 1996, reproduced by permission of the author

'Supper time', 'Sing a song of sixpence', 'Eight cakes' and 'One, two, three, four, five', from *Nonsense counting rhymes* by Kaye Umansky, Oxford University Press 1999, reproduced by kind permission of Kaye Umansky, c/o Caroline Sheldon Literary Agency.

'My grannies' by June Crebbin from *Bags of Poems: Family Album*, compiled by Jill Bennett, Corgi 1995, reprinted by permission of the author.

'Grandpa never sleeps' by Mark Burgess, from *Bags of Poems: Family Album*, compiled by Jill Bennett, Corgi 1995.

'Friends again' by Paul Rogers from *Bags of Poems: Family Album*, compiled by Jill Bennett, Corgi 1995, reprinted by permission of the author.

'My little sister' by Ann Bonner from *Bags of Poems: Family Album*, compiled by Jill Bennett, Corgi 1995, © Ann Bonner 1988, first published by Scholastic in *Infant Projects*, reproduced by permission of the author.

List of Assessment Focuses

Assessment focus	Chapter	Date achieved/comments
Can the child relate to stories about own experiences, understand story structure, identify capital letters at the beginning of sentences and recognise high frequency words?	1	
Can the child tell the difference between spoken and written forms, recognise if simple sentences make sense and recognise alphabet letters and alphabetical order?	2	
Can the child predict the meaning of unfamiliar words, recognise full stops, and recognise and name initial and final phonemes in c-v-c words?	3	
Can the child understand rhymes and rhyming patterns, identify rhyming words or phrases, create rhyming families and appreciate familiar and traditional rhymes?	4	
Can the child identify rhythm patterns and write simple poems with identifiable rhyme and rhythm patterns?	5	
Can the child identify the sequence of a story, predict words in a sentence that 'fit' and make sense and identify, spell and read all phonemes in a c-v-c- word?	6	
Can the child analyse characters in a story, use the term 'sentence' appropriately and identify initial consonant clusters?	7	
Can the child identify story themes, use capital letters for names and spell words with 's' for plurals?	8	
Can the child recite action poems and use action poems for own writing of new lines?	9	
Can the child recognise familiar poems that are written with a new slant and write own simple poems from other familiar poems?	10	
Can the child use the title page and blurb of a book to judge its content, reorder sentences to make sense and use spellings with 'ed' for the past tense?	11	
Can the child appreciate stories with a familiar setting, use capital letters for personal titles and recognise high frequency words?	12	
Can the child appreciate fantasy stories, use question marks appropriately and use the terms 'vowel' and 'consonant' correctly?	13	
Can the child appreciate poems on the same theme, relate a theme to own experiences and use the poetry for own writing?	14	
Can the child analyse traditional poems in depth and use them as models for own work by substituting words and elaborating on the text?	15	

Stories about own experiences

Overall aims

- To relate the events in the story to the children's own lives.
- To understand story structure.
- To identify capital letters at the beginning of sentences.
- To consolidate some of the high frequency words.

Featured book

Poor Monty by Anne Fine

Story synopsis

Monty's mother is a very busy doctor, juggling a hectic working life with home life. At the end of her hectic day, all she wants to do is have a few quiet minutes, reading the paper and drinking a cup of tea. Monty isn't feeling very well and he has a hard job trying to tell his mother, who is engrossed in the paper. Only when he bursts into tears and bawls aloud does Monty's mother realise that her little boy is unwell. Then, of course, she cuddles him and puts him to bed, to nurse him better.

Lesson One

Intended learning

- To relate the events in the story to the children's own experiences.
- To understand the structure of a story.

With the whole class

- Introduce the story to the children. Read the title, show them the cover and ask what they think the book might be about.
- Ask them to say why they think Monty is 'poor', judging from the front cover.
- Then read the story to the children. Ask whether this has happened to any of them. Encourage them to share their experiences. Discuss their feelings when they felt unwell. How would they feel if they were ignored?

Agree words to describe these feelings and write them on the board.

- Ask the children whether this story is just about Monty. What do they think Monty was doing when his mother was at work?
- Explain that all stories have a beginning, a middle and an end, in order to make sense. Ask the children to tell the beginning part of *Poor Monty*, showing them the pictures to jog their memories. Ask them what the middle part is about, again showing the pictures. Finally, ask them to tell the end of the story.
- Ask them to name a favourite fairytale and discuss together its beginning, middle and end.

With the lower-achievers

With adult support
Choose from:

1 Look through the book together. (If possible, use multiple copies.) Discuss the pictures focusing on Monty's face. Ask the children how they think Monty is feeling, through the different stages of the story.

2 Divide a sheet of A4 into four for each child. Write 'happy', 'sad', 'busy' and 'surprised' in the sections. Look at the pictures in the book and ask the children to draw in each section a picture of whichever character best fits the descriptions.

3 Using Resource sheet 1a, ask the children to match the words to the pictures. Talk about the sequence of the pictures and how this is important for the story to make sense.

4 Ask the children to describe other life experiences, such as getting lost, losing a relative or pet, disliking school or going to hospital.

Teacher-independent activities
Choose from:

1 Ask the children to think of one of their life experiences and draw a picture of it. They should write on the picture whether this was a happy time, sad time and so on. Tell them to refer to the emotion words written on the board or have the words written on cards.

2 Ask the children to complete Resource sheet 1a.

3 Cut out the pictures from Resource sheet 1a before the lesson. Ask the children to stick them in sequence on card. If they are able they could write the words under the pictures.

4 Ask the children to work in pairs and go through the book again. Ask them to role-play the story.

Plenary session

■ Make up some sentences to tell the story on Resource sheet 1a and write them on the board in the wrong order. Read them with the children and ask them to say what order they should be in. Ask them for the beginning sentence first, followed by the middle sentences and finally the last sentence. Tell them the story of the pictures again, using the four sentences.

■ Talk about why stories have a beginning, a middle and an end. It would be strange if you started in the middle of the story and didn't know anything about the characters. Open *Poor Monty* in the middle and read from it. Is this the right place to start a story? Would the children feel happy if the story ended when Monty burst into tears?

■ Ask the children whether they felt sorry for Monty. Did they still feel sorry for him at the end of the story? Why or why not? Have they ever felt like Monty felt? Why?

Lesson Two
. . . .

Intended learning

■ To work with the text and the pictures to explore a range of emotion words.

■ To look at other books which deal with children's experiences.

■ To identify capital letters at the beginning of sentences.

With the whole class

■ Ask the children to remind you about the *Poor Monty* story.

■ Looking only at the pictures in *Poor Monty* ask the children how they think Monty and Monty's mother are feeling in each illustration.

■ Remind the children of the emotion words discussed and written up in Lesson One. Write them on the board again adding to them if necessary. Discuss each word and its meaning. Discuss what events might make people feel these emotions.

■ Referring to the book again, show the children the capital letters at the beginning of the sentences. Explain what they are and why they are used – to show us when a new sentence starts.

■ Write some different sentences on the board using the emotion words. Point out the capital letters at the beginning of each sentence.

With the lower-achievers
With adult support
Choose from:

1 Look again at the range of emotion words. Ask the children if they have felt any of these. If so, in what context? With an adult scribing if necessary, get them to write and draw about these words. Make a copy of Generic sheet 1 on page 117 and discuss with the children which different emotions are being shown.

2 Look at another book dealing with children's experiences (for example, *Dogger* by Shirley Hughes, *Changes* by Anthony Browne or *Where's my Mum?* by Leon Rosselson). Ask the children how they would feel if they were the child in the story.

3 Using a copy of *Poor Monty* or another story book, ask the children to find some capital letters and see if they can name them.

4 Using Resource sheet 1b, help the children to read the sentences and then to supply the missing capital letter for each sentence.

Teacher-independent activities

Choose from:

1   Use Resource sheet 1b to play a game. Enlarge enough copies of the sheet for each child in the group. Cut out the single letters from the top and mount them onto card. Mount the part of the sheet with the sentences onto card. Make a few extra capital letter cards that can't be used in the sentences. Place the single letters face down on the table and tell the children to take one, in turns. If it fits one of the sentences, they may keep it; if it is a 'false' letter, it must be returned to the bottom of the pile. The winner completes their sentences first.

2   Using Resource sheet 1b, ask the children to write out the sentences again on paper, including the capital letters. Ask them to draw their own picture to illustrate each sentence.

3   Give the children Generic sheet 1 on page 117 or find pictures in old magazines that show people who are happy, sad, scared and so on. Ask the children to cut out the pictures and stick them onto sheets of paper, writing the relevant emotion words on the board if they wish.

Plenary session

■   Ask the children who looked at other books to say which their favourites were and why. Do they know any other stories that are about life experiences?

■   Look again at the list of emotion words and discuss them with the children. Are there any of these words they don't understand? Can they think of some more emotion words?

■   Share Resource sheet 1b with the children. Ask for volunteers to say which capital letters belong to which sentences. Ask them to look around the room at the captions on the wall displays. Can they name the capital letters in these? Can they read the words with capital letters?

Lesson Three

Intended learning

■   To consolidate some of the high frequency words that appear in the text.

■   To recognise these high frequency words in other contexts.

With the whole class

■   Write on the board 'and', 'said', 'she' and 'was'. Read the words with the children several times.

■   Play 'Hangman' using these words. Draw dashes for each letter in the word. Write those that the children guess correctly in the right place on the dashes and those that they don't at the side, drawing each stage of the hangman's noose for every wrong letter. Can the children get the word before the person is hung?

■   Ask the children to look around the classroom and identify the words in display captions. For example, if a child's picture has the caption 'My mummy was happy. She had a birthday.', point out the words 'was' and 'she'. Can the children put the words into their own sentences orally?

■   Read part of *Poor Monty* with the children. Ask them to listen carefully for when each high frequency word appears. They could put up their hands when they hear one of the words.

With the lower-achievers

With adult support

Choose from:

1   Using Resource sheet 1c, ask the children to match the high frequency words to the correct sentences and then match the sentences to the pictures.

2   Giving help where needed, ask the children to make the high frequency words in as many different media as possible. For example, with sandpaper, with Plasticine sausages, by sticking pasta into outlines of the words, with stencils on coloured paper, by bending and sticking straws into the word shapes, by bending pipe-cleaners, and so on.

3   Ask the children to make their own sentences for the high frequency words and write them. Give help where necessary.

Teacher-independent activities

Choose from:

1   Copy Generic sheet 2 on page 118 several times and cut out the cards. Ask the children to play 'Snap' or 'Pelmanism' with the cards.

2   Using part of an old storybook of a suitable level, ask the children to circle in different colours each high frequency word, for example, red for 'and', blue for 'said', green for 'she' and yellow for 'was'. They could then write sentences using as many of these words as they can.

3   Copy Generic sheet 2 on page 118 several times and cut out the cards. Allocate a value to each word, for example, 'said' could have a value of 3, 'and' 2, 'she' 1 and 'was' 2. Write these values beside each word. Shuffle the cards and place them face down on the table. Each child takes a card and if they can read it they keep it. After a given time the game is ended and the children add up their values. The winner is the child with the highest total.

Plenary session

- Play a game to see who can take a 'photograph' of a word in their head, then write it on the board. Show individual children a card with the chosen word written on it and ask them to take a photograph of it in their head. They then come up to the board and write the word. This helps to develop the 'look, say, cover, write, check' method.

- Write on the board the first letter for each of the high frequency words followed by dashes for the other letters. Ask the children to say which high-frequency words they think they are. Let them come up and write the remaining letters in.

- Ask the children whether there is anything they don't understand about these high-frequency words.

■ Match the words to the pictures by drawing lines.

| run | | fall | | sad | | better |

■ Write the capital letter at the beginning
of each sentence.

T   D   C   M   W

___ogs like to bark.

___he boy is sad.

___e went out to play.

___y bike is big.

___an you see my car?

✏️ Write the missing words in the sentences.

The girl _____ in bed.

"I like chips," _____ the boy.

A dog _____ a cat played.

Mum said that _____ was happy.

| and |
| said |
| she |
| was |

■ Match the sentences to the pictures.

Stories for spoken and written forms

Overall aims

- To know the difference between spoken and written forms.
- To recognise whether simple sentences make sense.
- To practise and secure alphabet letter knowledge and alphabetical order.

Featured book

Funnybones by Janet and Allan Ahlberg

Story synopsis

The big skeleton, the little skeleton and the dog skeleton set out one dark night to frighten somebody. Unfortunately, they don't meet anybody so they have to amuse themselves another way. When the dog skeleton accidentally falls to pieces, the other two have to put him together again, which they eventually manage. They finally decide to frighten each other instead and do so all the way home, encountering a few dinosaur skeletons *en route*.

Lesson One

Intended learning

- To understand the difference between spoken and written forms through retelling known stories.
- To use the text and other familiar stories to compare the spoken and written versions.

With the whole class

- Read *Funnybones* to the children. Show them the text, pointing to the words as you read them. At the end, ask the children how you knew what words to say to tell the story. Point out that you had no choice of words when you were reading.
- Ask the children to tell the story of *Funnybones* in their own words. Ask how they knew what words to choose. Ask whether their words were the same as those in the book. Why were they able to use different words? Did the children

use direct or reported speech by the skeletons? Point this out to them. (At this stage, don't use these terms since this is addressed in Year 5.) Use explanations such as, *"Manjit said 'The skeletons decided to scare some people', but in the written story it says, '"Let's take the dog for a walk," said the little skeleton, "and frighten somebody!" "Good idea!" the big skeleton said."'* It is very important to assure the children that both versions are correct. Explain that written and spoken versions are only different, not right or wrong.

- Ask someone to choose a favourite book that everyone else knows as well, such as a collection of fairytales. Choose one of the stories and ask the children to tell it in their own words. Then read the story to them. Ask how the two versions were different. Again, reassure them that their spoken version is just as valid and acceptable.

With the lower-achievers

With adult support

Choose from:

1 Allocate roles to the children and ask them to act out the story of *Funnybones*. (This may need to be done away from the main classroom.) Discuss with them how this differs from the text or written form. Point out how they were able to choose their own words. Explain that they could not use the descriptive passages because they were acting the story. Ask if they could use describing words if they were only telling the story. Why?

2 Using Resource sheet 2a, ask the children to read the sentences and match them to the correct pictures. Then ask them to use a cassette recorder to tell the story in their own words. (If individual recorders are not available, the children could work in pairs or threes and take turns to tell each part of the story.) Work closely with the children to discuss how their spoken version is different from the written sentences. Ensure they understand that their version is equally acceptable.

3 Ask the children to use puppets or dolls to tell a favourite story. Ask them how this is different from the story as it is written. Point out how they are able to give the characters words to

speak that may not be identical to the written version, but are just as correct. Practise this for a class performance.

Teacher-independent activities

Choose from:

1   Using Resource sheet 2a, ask the children to match the correct sentences to the pictures. Ask them to work in pairs to tell the story into a cassette recorder, using their own words. This new version can then be shared with the other children when the group is brought together again.

2   Give pairs of children a copy of Generic sheet 3 on page 119. Ask them to work in their pairs to write a sentence about the story and then to practise telling it orally. When the group is brought together again, ask the children to present their two versions to the others and discuss how they differ.

3   Prepare some cassettes by recording known stories that have a written version available in the classroom. Ask the children to work in pairs and listen to your recorded version and then read the written version. Ask them to write a few sentences saying how the two versions are different. Share these at the plenary session.

Plenary session

■   Ask the children how the spoken and written versions of a story are different. Make a large chart and write their answers in bullet points. Leave this on the wall for reference while the point is still being taught.

■   Ask the children who worked on role-play and/or puppet versions of a story to give a performance of their version. Ask the rest of the class how this is different from a written version. Ensure they fully understand that both versions are valid and acceptable.

■   Ask the children who listened to a recorded story and then read the written version to share what they wrote about the different versions. Discuss this with the whole group.

Lesson Two

Intended learning

■   To recognise whether simple sentences make sense.

■   To work with wrong word order or missing words to check the sense of sentences.

With the whole class

■   Write on the board a simple sentence with the words in the wrong order. For example, 'Jack and Jill hill went the up.' Read this with the children and ask them whether it makes sense. Ask them why not.

■   Ask for volunteers to come to the board to write the sentence again in the correct order – each child could write one word. Read the sentence again with the class. Ask whether it makes sense this time.

■   Read a few sentences from *Funnybones* in the wrong order. For example, 'The big skeleton and skeleton little the swings on played the.' Ask the children to tell you how these should read to make sense.

■   Write on the board a simple sentence with a word missing. For example, 'Cinderella wanted to __ to the ball.' Read it with the children and ask whether it makes sense. Ask them why not. Ask for a volunteer to write the missing word on the board. Read the sentence again with the children and ask whether it makes sense this time.

■   Read a few sentences from *Funnybones* with a word or two missing. Ask the children to tell you what the missing words are for these to make sense.

With the lower-achievers

With adult support

Choose from:

1   Using Resource sheet 2b, ask the children to supply the missing words to complete the sentences, and to rewrite the sentences that are in the wrong order. You may have to help them

with the writing. Then ask them to match the sentences at the top of the page to the pictures.

2 Cut out and enlarge sentences from an old storybook, stick them onto card and then cut them into the individual words. These can be used to play two games. In the first game, present the children with the word cards and ask them to place these in the correct order. In the second game, present the words in order but with one (or, according to ability, two) words missing. Ask the children to supply a sensible missing word orally.

3 Prior to this activity, write on the board four or six sentences, half with a word missing and half in the wrong order. Working closely with the children, read the sentences together and ask them to supply the missing words and to write the muddled sentences in the correct order.

Teacher-independent activities

Choose from:

1 Enlarge copies of familiar nursery rhymes. Stick them onto card and cut them into the individual sentences. Ask the children to put the sentences in order to make the rhyme, then write out the rhyme and illustrate it.

2 A more challenging activity is to cut the rhymes up into individual words. (Keep each segmented sentence together in envelopes, numbered according to each line of the rhyme.) Ask the children to put the words into the correct order and write the sentence. According to ability, also ask them to place the sentences in the correct order to make the complete nursery rhyme.

3 Prepare a sheet with six or eight simple sentences, half of them with missing words or in the wrong order, and half making sense. (You could use the sentences from Resource sheet 2b.) Ask the children to put a tick beside the sentences that are sensible and a cross beside those which are not.

4 Ask the children to complete Resource sheet 2b.

Plenary session

■ Write two or three simple sentences on the board in the wrong order or with a word missing. Read these with the children. Ask for volunteers to write the correct sentence on the board.

■ Ask why sentences have to be written in the right order and why they need all the words.

■ Ask the children who worked with Resource sheet 2b to share with the class what they have learned. Ask them to explain what they did with their sentences.

■ Ask if there is anything they don't understand.

Lesson Three

Intended learning

■ To practise and secure alphabet letter knowledge and alphabetical order.

■ To use the chosen story to recognise letters and alphabetical order.

With the whole class

(Ensure there is an illustrated alphabet on display before doing this lesson, or make sure every child has a copy of Generic sheet 4 on page 120.)

■ Ask the children to remind you of the *Funnybones* story.

■ Using the story and the classroom alphabet as the basis, play a quick-fire game 'Which letter?' For example, ask *"What letter does 'dog' begin with?"* or *"What begins with 's'?"* (Ensure that both forms of the question are asked during the game.) Record their suggestions on the board. You could play this game against the clock. Encourage the children to beat their own record in subsequent games.

■ Write three or four words (from the alphabet display) on the board in any order and ask the children to name the initial letters. Ask them which word comes first in the alphabet. Write the words again in alphabetical order.

■ Write on the board 'big', 'skeleton', 'little' and 'dog'. Ask the children to put these into alphabetical order. Ask them to come to the board to write the words.

With the lower-achievers

With adult support

Choose from:

1 For further consolidation of letters, play games such as 'I Spy' and 'Grandma Went to Market'.

2 Ask the children to write their first names on the board. Then ask them to put the list into alphabetical order. (Use only the initial letter at this stage, unless second letters can't be avoided because of duplicate initial letters.) Do the same with their family names. Can they tell you some of the letters of the alphabet they did not use? Let them refer to Generic sheet 4 (page 120) for help in identifying the letters.

3 Write the words 'initial letter' on the board and read it to the children. Tell them what it means. Give them copies of Resource sheet 2c and read the instructions with them. They should write under each picture its initial letter. They then put the pictures into alphabetical order and write the words and finally write the name of the object that begins with a given letter. Give support where necessary.

4 Ask the children to collect small items from around the classroom and place these in a display on the windowsill in alphabetical order. With the children, make labels for the items, writing the initial letter in a different colour.

Teacher-independent activities

Choose from:

1 Ask the children to read the labels in the classroom, for example, 'door', 'library', 'table', 'window', and write them in alphabetical order.

2 Let the children complete the activities on Resource sheet 2c.

3 Ask the children to work in pairs and give each pair a 'feely bag' containing a few items such as a small doll, a toy fish, a spoon and so on. Ask the children to write in alphabetical order a list of their bag's contents. If they cannot write the

words they could draw pictures of the objects in alphabetical order.

4 Ask the children to collect as many things as they can, beginning with a given letter. Ask them to write a list. Give each child a different letter.

5 Before the lesson have prepared a copy of Generic sheet 4 stuck onto card and cut up into individual pictures. Give a few cards to each child and ask them to put them into alphabetical order. They should then write the words or draw the pictures in alphabetical order.

Plenary session

■ Give each child a letter tile (duplicating if necessary). Ask them to come to the front of the class in alphabetical order of their tiles.

■ Ask the children who made a collection of items for the windowsill to explain why these are in the given order.

■ Write several family names on the board and ask what the alphabetical order is. Ask different children to write the names again, in alphabetical order.

■ Ask the children if there is anything they don't understand about the alphabet letters and alphabetical order.

■ Read the sentences. Match them to the pictures.

Goldilocks saw a house in the woods.

She ate the baby bear's porridge.

She went to sleep in the baby bear's bed.

The three bears saw Goldilocks in the bed.

■ Now tell the story. Use a tape recorder.

Write the missing words in these sentences.
Then match the sentences to the pictures.

house	ran	big	to

The boy was going _____ school.

My cat _____ up a tree.

Mum made a _____ cake.

We live in a big _____ .

 The words in these sentences are mixed up.
Write the sentences so they make sense.

shops. went the We to

_____

dad football. My play can

_____

boy the played The dog. with

_____

Write the initial letter under each picture.

_____   _____   _____

_____   _____   _____

 Write the words in alphabetical order.

1. _____   2. _____

3. _____   4. _____

5. _____   6. _____

 What begins with d? _____

What begins with t? _____

What begins with m? _____

Stories for unfamiliar words

Overall aims

- To use the text and illustrations of a story to predict the meaning of unfamiliar words.

- To recognise full stops and name them correctly.

- To recognise and name initial and final phonemes in c-v-c words.

Featured book

Terrible Tuesday by Hazel Townson and Tony Ross

Story synopsis

Terry overhears his mother on the phone saying how scared she is about the coming Tuesday. He imagines all kinds of disasters and terrifying happenings, from space invasions to hurricanes, from kidnappings to bank robberies. When Terrible Tuesday finally arrives the event turns out to be Terry's favourite cousins coming for tea. For Terry, this is great, but for Terry's mum, the illustration shows why she dreaded the day, as an adult reader will instantly recognise!

Lesson One

Intended learning

- To study the text and the illustrations to predict the meaning of unfamiliar words.

- To generalise this strategy to other texts/stories.

With the whole class

- Read the story with the children but before reading the text on each page, discuss the illustrations and ask them to predict what event might happen on Terrible Tuesday.

- Look at the page where Terry imagines himself being kidnapped and discuss with the children what is happening to Terry. Why are the police chasing the men who have taken Terry? Why are there a helicopter and a police car joining the chase? Do the children know the word 'kidnap'? Write it on the board.

- Look at the page showing the imaginary flood. Can the children explain that the water deluging the town is because of the heavy rain? Do they know the word 'flood'? Write it on the board.

- Discuss the illustration of the bank robbery. Why are there men outside the bank holding Terry's dad at gunpoint? Why is their car so close to the building? Do the children know the words 'foil' and 'hero'? Do they know what they mean? Can they tell you this from the sentence, 'Fancy seeing your own dad on the television news!'? Write the words on the board.

- Ask the children what the picture on the opposite page shows. Can they tell you what 'gagged' means by looking at the picture and reading the accompanying sentence? Write 'gagged' on the board.

- Explain the definitions to them. Write the words onto cards to use as flash cards. Also list them on a large sheet of paper to display on the wall, for reference while working on this lesson.

- When you have finished reading the story, ask the children why Tuesday was so terrible for Terry's mum, when Terry thought it was a good day. If necessary, discuss the illustrations and explain how and why the adults would see this event very differently!

With the lower-achievers

With adult support

Choose from:

1 Using the flash cards from the whole-class session, ask the children if they can remember what the words are. Remind them if necessary and tell them again the definitions of the words. Ask them what part of the story each word appeared in. Can they put the words in the order that they appeared in the story?

2 Using Resource sheet 3a and working closely with the children, help them to write the definition for each word. Then help them to look in a dictionary for the definitions. (Make sure they can see an alphabet.) Discuss with them whether their definitions were similar to the dictionary's.

3   Read a different story with the children, using multiple copies if possible. Encourage them to work out the meanings of unfamiliar words then check them in a dictionary. Encourage the children to use the illustrations to help them to work out the meanings of the unfamiliar words.

Teacher-independent activities

Choose from:

1   Ask the children to use dictionaries to help them complete Resource sheet 3a. They may need to work in pairs.

2   Using the flash cards from the whole-class session, ask the children to choose two of the words to learn by looking at the word, saying it aloud and then turning the card over before writing the word. How many turns do they need before writing the word without any mistakes? Can they beat an egg-timer, for example?

3   Ask the children to work in pairs and read the first two or three pages of another story. Ask them to write down any unfamiliar words they find and what they think these might mean. Ask them to check the meanings in a dictionary.

Plenary session

■ Discuss with the children what strategies they used to find the meanings of unfamiliar words. Some suggestions might include using the illustrations, using a dictionary, using the general context of the story, reading on and going back afterwards to check the meaning.

■ Ask the children who read another story to share their unfamiliar words with the class and say how accurate their definitions were.

■ Ask for volunteers to write on the board some of the words from the whole-class session, spelling these unaided if possible.

Lesson Two

Intended learning

■ To recognise full stops and name them correctly.

■ To use several types of text to generalise the concept of using full stops at the end of sentences.

With the whole class

■ Write a simple sentence on the board with the full stop in a different colour. Read the sentence with the children. Point to the full stop and ask if they know what it is called. Write 'full stop' on the board. Ask the children if they know what it is for.

■ Explain that its job in this case is to show us where a sentence ends. On the board, write a sentence related in some way to the first and give it a full stop at the end. Then read aloud the two sentences, exaggerating the pause at the end of the first sentence. Read them again without pausing at the full stop. Do the children see that the full stop helps the sentences to make sense?

■ Can the children tell you where they will find full stops? List their suggestions. They may say, for example, books, magazines, comics, newspapers, brochures and so on. Ask them to look around the classroom and identify labels, captions, posters and so on that have full stops.

■ Ask for volunteers to choose a page of *Terrible Tuesday* at random and show you the full stops on it. (Most pages have at least two.) Then show full stops on these pages to the whole class.

■ You could play a game where the children shout out when you come to a full stop when reading some pages from *Terrible Tuesday*.

With the lower-achievers

With adult support

Choose from:

1 Write several simple sentences on the board without a full stop. Read these with the children. Can they tell you what's missing? Ask for volunteers to come and put in the full stops. Give them a different colour to do this. Ask them again to identify by name the full stops.

2 Using Resource sheet 3b, ask the children to read the sentences and put the full stops in the correct places. Ask them to then complete the unfinished sentences using the words at the bottom of the sheet. Remind them to put in the full stops.

3 Look at the first two or three pages of *Terrible Tuesday* together. Ask the children to identify the full stops. Can they tell you why the sentences have full stops? If necessary, repeat the name and the function of full stops. Can they show you some more sentences ending in full stops in the book?

Teacher-independent activities

Choose from:

1 Enlarge a short piece of text from a book of an appropriate reading level and ask the children to work in pairs to read through it and identify the full stops. Ask them to circle these with a coloured pen and then write a sentence of their own and use a full stop at the end.

2 Ask the children to complete Resource sheet 3b.

3 Enlarge Resource sheet 3b, stick it onto card and cut the sentences into individual words (or make your own word cards). Make several 'full stop' cards. Put the words from each sentence and a full stop card into separate envelopes. Ask the children to work in pairs to put the cards in the correct order, to make the sentence, including the full stop. Ask them to write the sentences.

Plenary session

■ Write on the board 'full stop' and ask the children what it says. Ask for volunteers to go and point to examples of full stops they can see in the classroom.

■ Ask some of the children who completed Resource sheet 3b to show the other children their sentences, now complete with full stops. Can they read these to the class?

■ Write two or three simple sentences on the board without full stops. Can the children tell you what's missing? Ask for volunteers to come and put in the full stops.

■ Ask if there's anything about full stops they don't understand.

Lesson Three

Intended learning

■ To revise the terms 'phoneme', 'initial' and 'final' from Reception Year.

■ To recognise and name initial and final phonemes in c-v-c words.

With the whole class

■ Remind the children of the words 'phoneme', 'initial' and 'final' that they learned in Reception Year. Can they tell you what each of these means? Write the words on the board and read them out loud with the children.

■ Using picture cards for clues, emphasise the initial phonemes of some objects. Can the children tell you the sound? For example, *"What is the initial phoneme of 'cat'?"* or *"What is the initial phoneme of 'peg'?"*

■ Again, using picture cards for clues, emphasise the final phonemes of the objects. Can the children tell you the sound? For example, *"What is the final phoneme of 'dog'?"* or *"What is the final phoneme of 'tap'?"*

■ Display each picture on the board. Can any of the children write on the board the initial and final phonemes under each one? (Use one colour for the initial phonemes and another for the final phonemes.)

With the lower-achievers

With adult support

Choose from:

1 Have prepared a tape of c-v-c words to go with the set of pictures on Resource sheet 3c, emphasising first the initial and then the final phonemes. Ask the children to listen to the tape and point to the picture of the word as it is spoken.

2 Using Resource sheet 3c, ask the children to identify and write the initial and final phonemes of the illustrated c-v-c words. If necessary, give support by saying the words with the emphasis on the appropriate phoneme.

3 Working closely with the children, look through *Terrible Tuesday* and find some of the c-v-c words. Can they tell you the initial and final phonemes of these? Encourage them to write the words using, for example, red for the initial phonemes and blue for the final phonemes.

4 Enlarge and cut out the pictures from Resource sheet 3c and place them face down on the table. The children should take a card and have to name the initial or final phonemes or both, as required. If they are correct, they may keep the card. The winner has the highest number of cards at the end of the game. Ask them to write a sentence using one of the words.

Teacher-independent activities

Choose from:

1 Give the children copies of Resource sheet 3c. Ask them to use a tape recorder to record themselves saying each word. Ask them to try to emphasise the sounds of the initial and final phonemes. They could do this in pairs.

2 Give the group the list of words written on paper during the whole-class session in Lesson One (kidnap, flood, foil, herp and gagged). Ask them to work in pairs to find these words in *Terrible Tuesday*. Give them a set of plastic letters and ask them to find all the initial phonemes in

one colour and all the final phonemes in another. They should make a display of these with the words next to them. Alternatively they could copy them out in different colours using crayons.

3 Using Resource sheet 3c, ask the children to identify and write the initial and final phonemes of the illustrated c-v-c words. Ask them to write a sentence for some of the words on the back of the sheet.

4 Enlarge and cut out the pictures from Resource sheet 3c and place them face down on the table. The children have to take a card and write the initial or final phonemes or both, as required.

Plenary session

■ Hold up the picture cards and ask for volunteers to tell you the initial and final phonemes of each. Can any of the children write these on the board?

■ Divide the class into two 'football teams' (of the children's choice) and play 'Phoneme Football'. Using the picture cards, a goal is scored when the correct phoneme (either initial, final or both) is identified. How many goals can each team score in five minutes?

■ Ask the children who completed Resource sheet 3c to show the class what they did. Can the other children name the initial and final phonemes of the words?

Name ______________________

Resource sheet 3a

■ Read these words.

kidnap	flood	foil	hero	gagged

Write what you think each word means.

kidnap ______________________

____

flood ______________________

____

foil ______________________

____

hero ______________________

____

gagged ______________________

____

■ Look for the words in a dictionary.
Were you right?

✏️ Put full stops at the ends of these sentences.

The children are going to school The boy has a football The girl has a skipping rope At playtime they will play with their toys

✏️ Finish these sentences using the words. Don't forget the full stops.

Humpty Dumpty sat on a _____

Jack and Jill went up the _____

The mouse ran up the _____

The cow jumped over the _____

| clock | hill | wall | moon |

✏ Write the initial phonemes for each picture.

____ ____ ____ ____

✏ Write the final phonemes for each picture.

____ ____ ____ ____

✏ Write the initial and final phonemes for each picture.

__ __ __ __ __ __ __ __

Poems for understanding rhymes

Overall aims

- To explore and understand rhymes and rhyming patterns.
- To identify rhyming words or phrases.
- To be able to create rhyme families through an understanding of rhymes and rhyming patterns.
- To revisit familiar and traditional rhymes.

Featured poems

Selected traditional rhymes.

Lesson One

Chosen poems

'Little Jack Horner' and 'Molly, my sister, and I fell out' – both traditional. (See page 30)

Intended learning

- To revisit traditional and familiar rhymes.
- To explore and understand rhymes.
- To be able to identify rhyming families.

With the whole class

- Enlarge copies of 'Little Jack Horner sat in a corner' and 'Molly, my sister, and I fell out'.
- Read 'Little Jack Horner' with the children and ask how many of them know it. Read it again with the children, pointing to each word as you do so.
- Ask the children what they notice about the ends of the lines. Explain what 'rhyme' means and point out that this is why nursery rhymes are so-called. Ask the children to name the rhyming words in 'Little Jack Horner'. Write them on the board. Can the children think of any other words that rhyme with these? For example, 'pie' and 'I' rhyme with 'eye', 'sky', 'try' and 'why'.
- Ask the children if they can remember any traditional/nursery rhymes. Encourage them to

recite or sing the rhymes. Write the rhyming words from the offered rhymes on the board. Ask for any other words that rhyme with these.

- Read 'Molly, my sister, and I fell out'. Ask the children to tell you the rhyming words in this poem. Ask them for other words to rhyme with these. For example, 'out' and 'about' also rhyme with 'shout', 'spout' and 'trout'.

With the lower-achievers

With adult support

Choose from:

1 Look through a nursery rhyme book together and find the rhyming words in two or three selected poems.

2 Using Resource sheet 4a, read the nursery rhyme with the children. Ask them to tell you which words rhyme. Then read the words around the poem. Ask the children to match those words to the appropriate rhyming words in the poem.

3 Make individual books dedicated to poetry, the covers illustrated by the children. (These can be used for poetry work throughout the year.)

4 Make a set of 'Snap'/'Pelmanism' cards with rhyming words. Play the games with the children, giving support to identify the rhyming words if necessary.

Teacher-independent activities

Choose from:

1 Ask the children to draw a large picture of their favourite rhyme and then try to write the rhyming words along the bottom of the picture.

2 Ask the children to look through two or three chosen poems and find the rhyming words. Ask them to write the words in a list using a different coloured pen for each set of rhyming words.

3 Using Resource sheet 4a, ask the children to match the rhyming words. Can they find more words that rhyme with the words on the sheet? They could write these on the back of the sheet.

Plenary session

■ Write on the board 'hat', 'peg' and 'tin'. How many words can the children think of that rhyme with each? Encourage them to come and write the words on the board.

■ Can the children think of words that rhyme with some of their names? For example, 'Sam' rhymes with 'ham', 'jam' and 'slam'. Write the rhymes on the board.

■ Ask the groups who found rhyming words in poems to share these with the whole class.

■ Ask if there is anything about rhyming that they haven't understood.

Lesson Two

Chosen poems

'A wise old owl' and 'I often sit and wish' – both traditional (See pages 30 and 31)

Intended learning

■ To consolidate the concept of rhyme and rhyming families.

■ To be able to create rhyme families through an understanding of rhymes and rhyming patterns.

■ To revisit familiar and traditional rhymes.

With the whole class

■ Enlarge copies of 'A wise old owl' and 'I often sit and wish'.

■ Read 'A wise old owl' with the children pointing to the text. Ask them what the rhyme is about. Ask them to identify the rhyming words and write these on the board in two columns. Can they think of any other words that rhyme with them?

■ Read 'I often sit and wish' with the children pointing to the text. Read it again, this time pausing before the end of each second line. Ask the children to supply the missing rhyme.

■ Ask the children what they would choose to be. (Not a kite!) From their answers, write associated words on the board. Ask the children for words that rhyme with these.

With the lower-achievers

With adult support

Choose from:

1 Play a game of 'Grandma Went to Market'. The objects she buys have to rhyme. Use endings such as 'at' or 'en', which give more rhyme opportunities.

2 Choose favourite rhymes and act them out. (This could be done away from the main classroom.) Ask the children for the rhyming words from each rhyme.

3 Make giant Rhyme Family posters. Write on them all the rhyming words that the children can think of and find.

4 Give the children a copy of Resource sheet 4b. Work closely with them to help them to match the pictures to the correct words and then to find the rhyming words.

Teacher-independent activities

Choose from:

1 Ask the children to make their own rhyme family lists. They may need 'starter words' to give them a base rhyme for each family. For example, 'mat', 'tin' and 'hen'. These could be written inside an appropriate shape such as a mat or a hen.

2 Ask the children to complete the activities on Resource sheet 4b.

3 Using Resource sheet 4b, ask the children to cut out the pictures and stick them onto large sheets of paper, one sheet to each rhyme. Ask them to write on each sheet other words that belong to that rhyming family. Can they find pictures of rhyming objects in old magazines to stick onto the sheets?

4 Using Resource sheet 4c, make word circles. Ask the children to make as many rhyming words as they can.

Plenary session

■ Ask the children who completed Resource sheet 4c to write on the board the words they made with their word wheels. Can the other children think of more rhyming words to go with these?

■ Can the children think of words that rhyme with the names of their clothes? For example, 'shoe' rhymes with 'blue', 'true' and 'screw'. Write the rhymes on the board.

■ Ask if there is anything about rhyming that they haven't understood.

Little Jack Horner

Sat in a corner,

Eating a Christmas pie;

He put in his thumb

And pulled out a plum,

And said, "What a good boy am I!"

Molly, my sister, and I fell out,
And what do you think it was all about?
She loved coffee and I loved tea,
And that was the reason we could not agree.

A wise owl lived in an oak;

The more he saw the less he spoke;

The less he spoke the more he heard.

Why can't we all be like that wise old bird?

All traditional

I often sit and wish that I

Could be a kite up in the sky,

And ride upon the breeze and go

Whatever way it chanced to blow;

Then I could look beyond the town,

And see the river winding down,

And follow all the ships that sail,

Like me, before the merry gale,

Until like them at last I came

To some place with a foreign name.

Traditional

■ Match all the words that rhyme.

blue   more   wait

picks   men

 One, two, buckle my shoe;

Three, four, shut the door;

Five, six, pick up sticks;

 Seven, eight, shut the gate;

Nine, ten, a big brown hen.

late   pen   floor

licks   true

■ Match the words that rhyme.

| cat | leg |

| bin | men |

| peg | hat |

| pen | pin |

■ Draw the other pictures.

✂ Cut out the circles.
Join them together with a split pin.

■ Make as many rhyming words as you can.

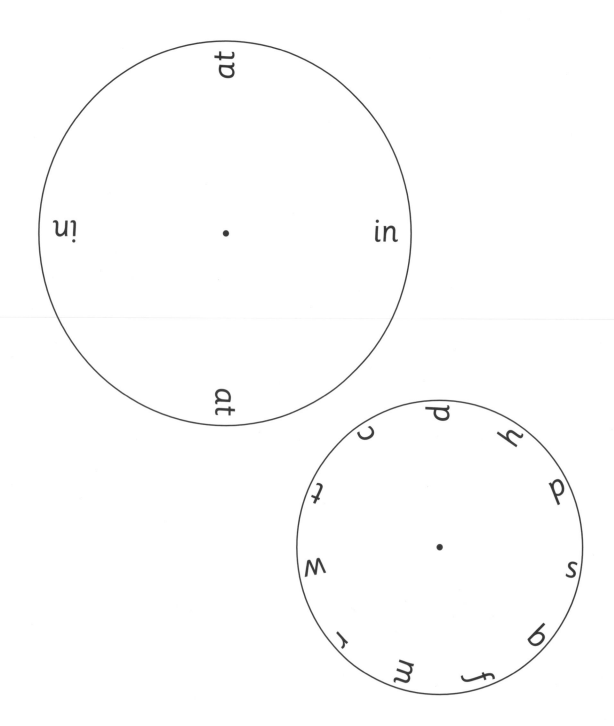

Poems with patterns

Overall aims

- To read several poems with different patterns of rhyme.
- To become aware of these different patterns.
- To explore rhythm in different poems.
- To write simple poems with identifiable patterns of rhyme and rhythm.

Featured books

Over and Over Again by Christopher Rowe and Barbara Ireson

Action Rhymes by John Foster

Lesson One

Chosen poems

'If', 'Sing a song of work to do' by Barbara Ireson and Christopher Rowe and 'This Old Man' – traditional (See pages 38 and 39)

Intended learning

- To explore several poems with different patterns of rhyme.
- To identify these patterns.
- To use the patterns as models for own compositions.

With the whole class

- Enlarge the poems 'If', 'Sing a song of work to do' and 'This Old Man'.
- Read 'If' with the children, pointing to the words. Ask them what the poem is about. Remind them what they have learned about rhyming words and ask them to identify which words in the poem rhyme.
- Repeat this for the other two poems. (Note – when discussing rhyming patterns, at this stage use only the rhyming examples – teaching the a, b, c format will be done later.) Tell the children that all these poems have patterns which they are going to look for.

- Discuss what the patterns might be. Explore the following ideas. 'If' has alternate rhyming lines in the pattern a, b, c, b. It has alternate lines that start with 'If I could' until the penultimate line. It has only one verse of eight lines. 'Sing a song of work to do' has a rhyming pattern a, a, b, b, c, c. It has three verses of six lines each. The last two lines of each verse are always the same. Each line starts with '... has to'. 'This Old Man' has ten verses of two lines. It has a chorus repeated after each verse and its rhyming pattern (a, a) is predictable, following a numerical sequence.
- Show the children how to use the patterns for their own compositions. For example, ask them for alternative line endings for 'This Old Man'.

With the lower-achievers

With adult support

Choose from:

1 Revisit each poem, encouraging the children to join in by saying the rhyming words at the appropriate points. Ask them to tell you what the pattern is in each poem. Remind them if necessary.

2 Using old newspapers, ask the children to cut out single words from the headlines, stick them on a sheet of paper and write a rhyming word for each one. Give support where necessary.

3 Read 'Sing a song of work to do', asking the children to offer alternative rhyming lines. For example, 'Martin has to paint his boat, Mary has to milk the goat'.

4 Using Resource sheet 5a, ask the children to finish the verses of 'This Old Man'. Reinforce the rhyming pattern of the poem.

5 Using copies of Generic sheet 8 on page 124, help the children to make big butterflies and write rhyming words on the underside of the wings. Hang them from the ceiling.

Teacher-independent activities

Choose from:

1 Using the enlarged copies of the poems, ask the children to put coloured circles around each rhyming word, using different colours for

different pairs of words. Challenge them to think of two more rhyming words for each pair.

2   Make a collection of word cards with words that rhyme with 'drum', 'shoe', 'knee' and 'door'. Ask the children to work in pairs to sort the cards into four piles, then turn the piles face down. Ask them to say the first four verses of 'This Old Man' and as they come to the end of the second line in each verse, not to say the word from the rhyme but to pick up a card from the pile and say that word instead. They should repeat this until all the cards are used. Can they think of some words to end the verses?

3   Ask the children to draw pictures to illustrate one verse of 'This Old Man', 'Sing a song of work to do' or 'If'. They could then write the rhyming words along the bottom of their picture.

Plenary session

■   Look again at the enlarged copy of 'If' and ask the children to tell you its rhyming pattern. Do the same for 'Sing a song of work to do' and 'This Old Man'.

■   Ask the children to choose a favourite nursery rhyme and recite it, thinking carefully about its rhyming pattern. Can they tell you what this is?

■   Using an enlarged copy of Resource sheet 5a, agree a class version of the poem. Write the new words on the sheet and display it.

Lesson Two

Chosen poems

'If I were a king' and 'If you should meet a giant' both by Barbara Ireson, and 'Pick 'N' Mix Zoo' by Celia Warren(See page 40.)

Intended learning

■   To explore rhythm in different poems.

■   To write simple poems with identifiable patterns of rhyme and rhythm.

With the whole class

■   Remind the children of the work they did on poems with patterns. Tell them that they are going to look at some different patterns now. Explain that they are going to explore the rhythms in the poems.

■   Ask the children if they know what 'rhythm' means. Explain that all words have rhythm and that poetry uses words in a rhythmic way.

■   Begin by encouraging the children to clap out and chant their names, street names, siblings' names and so on. Expand the chants to names and addresses, for example, *"Jaswinder lives in Barratt Street"* and *"Amanda goes home to Derwent Avenue"*.

■   Enlarge copies of 'If I were a king', 'If you should meet a giant' and 'Pick 'N' Mix Zoo'. Read the poems to the children, simultaneously clapping out their rhythms.

■   Read each poem again, encouraging the children to join in and to clap the rhythms at the same time. Discuss each poem's rhythm. Can they tell you how many beats there are in each line of the poems? Write the number alongside the lines on the enlarged copies.

With the lower-achievers

With adult support

Choose from:

1   Use musical instruments to beat out the rhythms of names and addresses and then the

rhythm of the poems. (This can be done away from the main classroom.)

2   Using Resource sheet 5b, ask the children to write their own poems. If necessary, read the words with them and help them to choose the words for their own poems. Read the poems together tapping out their rhythms.

3   Reread the chosen poems, clapping out the rhythms. Encourage the children to join in. Discuss again with the children each poem's rhythm. Can they tell you how many beats there are in each line of the poems? If necessary, look again at the enlarged copies.

4   Using Resource sheet 5c, ask the children to tap out the nursery rhyme and write down the number of taps it needs. If necessary, give more practice in this before writing anything on the sheet.

Teacher-independent activities

Choose from:

1   Ask the children to write their own poems using Resource sheet 5b. Encourage them to make a classroom poetry book using their sheets.

2   Ask the children to copy out their favourite two lines from 'Sing a song of work to do', except for the last words in each line. Challenge them to finish the lines with their own rhyming words.

3   Using Resource sheet 5c, ask the children to tap out the nursery rhyme and write down the number of taps it needs.

4   Working in pairs the children could think up different descriptions for the animals in 'Pick 'N' Mix Zoo'.

Plenary session

■   Ask the children who wrote new lines for 'Sing a song of work to do' to share their poems with the whole class. Can the other children identify the rhythms of the 'new' poems?

■   Ask the children who worked independently to write their own poems using Resource sheet 5b, to read these to the rest of the class. Leave the classroom poetry book that they made on display for reading in quiet moments.

If

If I could walk on the ceiling
The way that spiders do,
If I could hop for miles and miles
Just like a kangaroo,
If I could fly like a blackbird,
Or swim like a fish in the sea,
I'd be a funny person;
In fact, I wouldn't be me!

Christopher Rowe

Sing a song of work to do

Sing a song of work to do
Mother has to make a stew,
Grandpa has to mend a dish,
Grandma has to cook some fish,
And I've been busy all day long
Writing down this little song.

Martin has to paint his boat,
Mary has to mend her coat,
Simon has to clean the shed,
Sally has to make her bed,
And I've been busy all day long
Writing down this little song.

Johnnie has to beat the mat,
Jennie has to feed the cat,
Mandy has to brush her hair,
Mother has to dust the chair,
And I've been busy all day long
Writing down this little song.

Barbara Ireson and Christopher Rowe

This old man

This old man, he played one,
He played nick-nack on my drum.

This old man, he played two,
He played nick-nack on my shoe.

This old man, he played three,
He played nick-nack on my knee.

This old man, he played four,
He played nick-nack on my door.

This old man, he played five,
He played nick-nack on my hive.

This old man, he played six,
He played nick-nack on my sticks.

This old man, he played seven,
He played nick-nack up in heaven.

This old man, he played eight,
He played nick-nack on my gate.

This old man, he played nine,
He played nick-nack on my spine.

This old man, he played ten,
He played nick-nack once again.

Chorus

Nick-nack paddy-wack, give a dog a bone.
This old man came rolling home.

Traditional

If I were a king

If I were a king
I would wear a crown of gold,
And all the people round me
Would do as they were told.

If I were a queen
I would have a golden bed
And there I'd eat my breakfast
With my crown upon my head.

Barbara Ireson

If you should meet a giant,
Don't say: 'You're very tall,'
Or he might take you in his hand
And say: 'You're very small!'

Barbara Ireson

Pick 'N' Mix Zoo

Marshmallow monkeys,
Crocodile drops,
Red jelly elephants,
Lion lollipops.

Caramel camels,
Butterscotch bears,
Toffee hippopotamus,
Chocolate hares.

Peppermint pandas,
Candy kangaroo,
Strawberry snakes,
at the Pick 'N' Mix Zoo.

Celia Warren

■ Choose a word or a picture to finish the poem.

thumb

This old man, he played one,
He played nick-nack on my _____

glue

This old man, he played two,
He played nick-nack on my _____

tree

This old man, he played three,
He played nick-nack on my _____

floor

This old man, he played four,
He played nick-nack on my _____

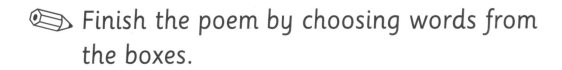 Finish the poem by choosing words from
the boxes.

I can _____,

You can _____,

We can _____ together!

sing	jump
sing	jump
sing	jump

Mum can't _____,

Dad can't _____,

They can't _____ together!

fly	dance
dance	fly
dance	fly

■ Now read your poem and tap the rhythm.

■ Tap the rhythm of the nursery rhyme.
Write in the boxes how many times you
tap for each line.

Jack and Jill went up the hill ☐

To fetch a pail of water. ☐

Jack fell down and broke his crown ☐

And Jill came tumbling after. ☐

Stories for sequencing

Overall aims

- To be able to identify the correct sequence of a storyline.
- To use preceding words in a sentence to predict words that 'fit' and make sense.
- To secure identification, spelling and reading of initial, medial and final letter sounds in c-v-c words.

Featured book

Burglar Bill by Janet and Allan Ahlberg

Story synopsis

Burglar Bill makes his living by going out at night and burgling houses, stealing anything that takes his fancy. He steals a box and gets more than he bargains for when he discovers it contains a baby. He has to look after the baby, feeding it, cleaning it and changing its nappy. One night, he realises that he himself is being burgled. The robber is Burglar Betty, who is, by coincidence, the baby's mum. She and Bill make friends and have a change of heart. They return all their stolen property, get married and settle down to a happy life of being honest.

Lesson One

Intended learning

- To be able to identify the correct sequence of a storyline.
- To work with the text, focusing on the beginning, the middle and the end of the story.
- To be able to generalise the concept of sequencing events.

With the whole class

- Ask the children to name a favourite story or fairytale. Ask how the story starts, what happens next, then what happens and how the story ends. Explain that all stories, events and daily living follow a sequence. Tell them they are going to learn the word 'sequence'.

- Read *Burglar Bill* with the children and then ask them what happened at the beginning. Explain that the character of Burglar Bill was introduced and that his way of life was described. Ask the children what two events happened in the middle of the story that were important, (finding the baby and being burgled by Burglar Betty). Ask the children how the story ended, (the wedding and the change of lifestyle for Betty and Bill).

- Write on the board three or four sentences outlining the sequence of an activity. (Baking a cake, getting ready for bed, buying a packet of crisps, making a cup of tea and so on.) Read these with the children. Then ask *"What order should these be in?"*

With the lower-achievers

With adult support

Choose from:

1 Ask the children to think about the order in which they get ready for school in the morning. Ask them to describe the order of undressing and dressing. Ask them to either write or draw this sequence.

2 Ask one child to retell the beginning of *Burglar Bill*, another the middle and a third the end. (Use the illustrations to jog memories if necessary.) Then ask the same children to tell the same part again, but this time ask them to speak so that the story is out of sequence. Can the others say whether that makes sense? What's wrong when we tell the story that way?

3 Using Resource sheet 6a, ask the children to cut out the pictures and put them into the correct sequence of the story. (If independent cutting out is not possible, give the pictures already cut.) As a group, with you acting as scribe, write the sequence in sentences.

4 Ask the children to act through the stages of *Burglar Bill* or another favourite story, both in sequence and mixed up. Which version makes sense? (If necessary, this activity can be done in a room away from the main class.) Ask them to practise this for the plenary session.

5 Using sequencing cards, such as those on Generic sheet 5 (page 121), encourage the

children to think carefully about correct order. Give each child one set of cards to sequence. Then display a set with one or two cards missing. Challenge the children to state which stage has been left out.

Teacher-independent activities

Choose from:

1   Cut out pictures from old comics, mix up the pictures and ask the children to reorder them in sequence.

2   Using Resource sheet 6a, ask the children to cut out the pictures and put them into the correct sequence of the story. Can they write short sentences to tell the story in sequence? Supply a word bank for them to choose from.

3   Ask the children to draw three or four large pictures representing the stages of *Burglar Bill*. Encourage them to move the sequence of pictures around until they acknowledge there is only one possibility. Ask them to write a sentence on each picture. Again supply a word bank for them to choose from.

4   Ask the children to write or draw the sequence of going for school lunch.

Plenary session

■   Remind the children how they found that the story of *Burglar Bill* followed a sequence of events. Use the book or pictures to recap, if necessary. Explain that all stories/situations are sequenced in a specific order, to make sense.

■   Ask the children who role-played *Burglar Bill* to give a performance of their play. Remind the other children to think about the sequence of the story while they are watching.

■   Can the children tell you the sequence of making a cup of tea, buying a loaf of bread and getting ready for bed?

Lesson Two

Intended learning

■   To use preceding words in a sentence to predict words that 'fit' and make sense.

■   To use different texts as a basis for practising predicting appropriate words.

With the whole class

■   Before the lesson, write on the board three or four simple sentences with a word missing in each. For example, 'Mum eats her breakfast in the _____ ', 'We can play in the _____', 'The _____ laid three eggs' and so on. Read these with the children. Can they suggest suitable words to complete the sentences? (For example, 'dining room/morning/ kitchen', 'playground/ park/garden' and 'hen/bird/snake'.) How did they know what words to suggest? (At this point, accept any suitable suggestions since there is no right or wrong answer.)

■   Explain that they have used the other words in the sentence to give them clues to the missing words. Can they offer alternative missing words? Do these make as much sense as their first choices? Why?/Why not?

■   Discuss good strategies for making good predictions, for example by reading to the end of sentences and looking at picture clues.

■   Read several sentences from *Burglar Bill* omitting one or two words. Challenge the children to supply sensible missing words. Are their words the same as those in the text? If not, do they change the meaning of the sentence?

With the lower-achievers

With adult support

Choose from:

1   Prior to this activity, write out a short piece of text from an old, favourite storybook leaving blanks for a few of the words. (No more than two or three sentences.) For example, 'The

third little _____ built a _____ of bricks. The wolf came to _____ it down.' Enlarge this and stick it onto card. Can the children read the sentences and supply sensible words for the missing parts? Ask them to write the text including their new words.

2 Using Resource sheet 6b ask the children to read the sentences and supply the missing words. They can use the suggestions on the sheet if they wish. Can they offer alternatives of their own? Give help if necessary.

3 Write on the board a few more sentences with missing words. Read these together and ask the children for suitable words to complete the sentences. Encourage them to write the words on the board themselves. Give support if necessary. Then have fun by asking them to think up funny alternatives, such as 'I went to school on a bus,' could be 'I went to school on an elephant.'

4 Read a short passage from a favourite book, pausing at suitable places. Encourage the children to supply appropriate words. How near to the original are their choices? Did their words still make sense?

Teacher-independent activities

Choose from:

1 Prior to this activity, blank off selected words on a page of an old comic using correcting fluid. (Ensure the comic is at an appropriate reading level.) Enlarge the page and give each child a copy. Ask them to read the storyline and write in suitable words where the blanks are.

2 Using Resource sheet 6b ask the children to read the sentences and supply the missing words. They can use the suggestions on the sheet if they wish. Can they offer alternatives of their own?

3 Prior to this activity, record onto a cassette several simple sentences, each with a word missing. Ask the children to listen to the tape and write down a suitable word for the one missing from each sentence. Alternatively, they could choose a word from a selection you have written on card for them. They can replay the tape to listen again as often as they like.

Plenary session

■ Ask the children who supplied missing words on either a resource sheet or a comic page, or for the cassette recording to share with the class what they did. How did they know what words to choose? Did they find it difficult?

■ Can the children tell you how they choose a suitable missing word? Agree that they use the other words in the sentence and the context of the story to make a decision.

■ Ask whether everybody understood what the work was about in this lesson. If necessary, spend a little more time practising the strategies taught.

Lesson Three

Intended learning

■ To secure identification, spelling and reading of initial, medial and final letter sounds in c-v-c words.

■ To revise the term 'medial' and consolidate the terms 'initial' and 'final'.

■ To use several texts to consolidate initial, medial and final letter sounds.

With the whole class

■ Write on the board several c-v-c words and ask for volunteers to read them. Can the children tell you what each word's initial, medial and final letter sound is? (At this point just indicate the letter you want and ask *"What phoneme does this letter make?"*)

■ Ask the children whether they can remember from the work they did in Reception year what the special name is for the position of the middle letter. If necessary, remind them and write on the board 'medial'. Can they tell you the proper names of the first and last phonemes? ('Initial' and 'final'.)

■ Ask individual children to come up and write on the board some c-v-c words of their own.

Challenge the others to identify the initial, medial and final letter phonemes of each word.

- Write up some c-v-c words with one of the letters missing and challenge the children to supply it. For example, '_ at' could be 'hat', 'bat', 'cat' and so on; 'p_n' could be 'pan', 'pen' or 'pin'; 'ca_' could be 'cat', 'cap', 'can' and so on.

- What do the children notice about the medial letter of every word? Can they remember the term 'vowel'? What are the vowels?

With the lower-achievers

With adult support

Choose from:

1 Look through *Burglar Bill* with the children, asking them to identify the c-v-c words and their initial, medial and final letter phonemes. You could write some of them out.

2 Prepare a sheet of A4 with several c-v-c words written on it. Ask the children to circle the initial letters in red, the medial letters in blue and the final letters in green. Can they write a sentence for each word?

3 Using Resource sheet 6c, ask the children to complete the words with either an initial, medial or final letter. Can they then match the words to the pictures? Ask them to read each word to you.

4 Give each child plastic letters including vowels. Ask them to make some c-v-c words using the letters.

Teacher-independent activities

Choose from:

1 Ask the children to work in pairs and play a form of 'Hangman' where only the initial, medial or final letter is missing. For example, '_in', 't_p' or 'ca_ '.

2 Using Resource sheet 6c, ask the children to complete the words with an initial, medial or final letter and then match the words to the pictures. Challenge them to write a sentence for each word on the back of the sheet.

3 Give the children a bag of plastic letters and a sheet of A4 divided into three sections titled

'initial', 'medial' and 'final'. Ask them to take letters from the bag and write them in one of the sections. (Remind them that only vowels are allowed in the 'medial' section.) How many real words can they make?

Plenary session

- Ask for volunteers to share with the others what they did. If they have sheets to show, encourage them to hold these up in view and talk about their tasks.

- Can they remember the terms for the beginning, middle and end letter sounds of c-v-c words? Write the words 'initial', 'medial' and 'final' on a large sheet of paper and leave it on display while working on this.

- Ask the children what they learned in this lesson. Was it new information or revision? What did they find hard? What did they find easy?

■ Cut out the pictures and put them in the right order.

✏️ Write a word to finish each sentence. You can use your own words or those in the boxes.

Every day I eat _____ .

The baby played with the _____ .

Mum put on her new _____ .

The boy drank all his _____ .

| milk | toys | dinner | dress |

✏️ Write some words to finish these sentences.

Dad made a big _____ .

The car went very fast along the _____ .

My dog had lots of _____ to eat .

I go to _____ every week .

✏️ Write the medial phonemes for the pictures.

  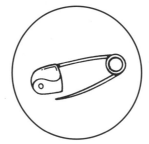 

h _ t   d _ g   p _ n   c _ p

✏️ Write the medial phonemes for the pictures.

___   ___   ___   ___

✏️ Write the missing phonemes and then match the words to the pictures.

   f _ n

                               _ e g

   c a ___

                               b _ n

Stories for characterisation

Overall aims

- To discuss main character(s) of a book and how the events of the story affect them.
- To use the term 'sentence' appropriately to identify sentences in texts.
- To identify initial consonant clusters.

Featured book

Backseat's Special Day by Scoular Anderson

Story synopsis

Backseat the dog waits patiently for his Special Day. Everyone else in the family has one, with presents and a cake, but his never seems to come. He tries to be friendly and helpful to make the family remember him and that he needs a Special Day, but everything he does goes wrong, especially when he tries to make his own Special Day cake. All ends well however when he raises the alarm during the night because the shed is on fire. The fire-fighters make such a mess in the kitchen that Backseat's mess is not noticed. He becomes the hero of the hour.

Lesson One

Intended learning

- To explore the chosen text and discuss aspects of characterisation in the story.
- To discuss how the events of the story affect the main character.

With the whole class

- Introduce the storybook to the children. Show them the cover and ask them what they think the book might be about. How do they think Backseat got his name? Read the story to them, showing them the text and the illustrations as you do so.
- Discuss the characterisation of Backseat. Consider the following points:

- ❏ the story is presented from Backseat's point of view
- ❏ although Backseat is a dog, the reader can empathise with him
- ❏ the speech bubbles from the family have words, but those from Backseat have pictures to express his needs/emotions etc, (don't draw attention to the speech bubbles as such here, since these are addressed in Year 2)
- ❏ he is innovative in attempting things to achieve his aim
- ❏ he is brave and persistent in raising the alarm when the fire breaks out
- ❏ he feels guilty about the mess in the kitchen so he hides
- ❏ he feels very happy when he finally has his Special Day.

- Ask the children to suggest words that describe Backseat. For example, 'sad', 'enthusiastic', 'frightened', 'happy' and 'worried'. Write the words on a large sheet of paper and display it for reference. You will need to read them to and with the children several times so that they recognise the shapes of the words, since sounding out some of these words will be too difficult at this stage.
- Do the children think Backseat changes between the beginning and the end of the story? How? Have the events of the story brought about this change? Did the fire have any effect on Backseat? How?

With the lower-achievers

With adult support

Choose from:

1   Read the story again, pausing at appropriate places to discuss with the children the aspects of Backseat's character that were talked about in the whole-class session.

2   Look at the words from the whole-class session that were written on the large sheet of paper. Read these with the children. Discuss each word and how it describes Backseat's character.

3   Prior to this activity, prepare a sheet of A4 for each child, divided into four. Ask the children to choose four words that describe Backseat, for example 'sad', 'enthusiastic', 'frightened', 'happy', 'worried' and so on. Write one word in each section of the paper. (Adult to scribe if necessary.) The children should then draw a picture of Backseat in each section to illustrate their chosen words. Ask them to make up sentences using these words.

4   Using Resource sheet 7a, ask the children to put a tick in the box next to the words that best describe Backseat. Give reading support if necessary. Explain that more than one word can be used to describe Backseat. Ask the children to complete the sentences at the bottom of the sheet.

Teacher-independent activities

Choose from:

1   Ask the children to draw a portrait of Backseat and write two or three words that describe him. (They could refer to the words on the large sheet of paper from the whole-class session.) If possible, they should write a sentence or two.

2   Ask the children to find other books that tell a story with an animal as the main character. Ask them to read these in pairs and discuss together what the main character is like. They should be able to tell the other children about this at the plenary session.

3   Make a set of flash cards with a word written on each that describes Backseat. (Use the words on the large sheet of paper from the whole-class session.) Place them face down in a pile. Working in pairs each child takes a card and tells his or her partner a sentence using that word.

4   Ask the children to choose an event from the story, for example how Backseat made his cake, or the fire. Ask them to draw and then label a picture about this and how Backseat reacted to the event.

Plenary session

■ Look at the words from the whole-class session that were written on the large sheet of paper. Read these with the children. Can they now add some new words to the list that also describe Backseat?

■ Ask the children who looked at other books with an animal as the main character to share with the other children what they thought the character was like.

■ Explain to the children that all stories have characters that we come to know through the way they behave or how the story affects them.

■ Ask the children whether there was anything they found difficult about discussing Backseat's character.

Lesson Two

Intended learning

■ To use the term 'sentence' appropriately to identify sentences in texts.

■ To revise the demarcation of a sentence by capital letters and full stops.

With the whole class

■ Write on the board two or three simple sentences and read them with the children. Ask them if they know what these lines of writing are called. Write 'sentence' on the board. Do the children know what it means? If necessary explain the term.

■ Point to the capital letter at the beginning and the full stop at the end of the sentence. Highlight these in a different colour. Explain that we use the word 'sentence' to describe a piece of writing that has a capital letter at the beginning and a full stop at the end and makes sense. Demonstrate this by writing or saying two sentences together without stopping at the full stop.

- Ask for volunteers to come to the front and look through *Backseat's Special Day* for a sentence. Ask them how they will know what they are looking for. Can they show their sentence to the other children? (Hold the book up while the child is pointing out the capital letter and full stop.)

- Ask the children to look around the room for other sentences. For example, captions accompanying pictures or displays. Can they go and point to the capital letters on their chosen examples?

With the lower-achievers

With adult support

Choose from:

1   Ensure the children have fully understood the term 'sentence'. Can they explain what it means? Can they identify a sentence correctly? If necessary, give them some more practice in using the term and in looking for capital letters and full stops.

2   Go through the text of another favourite book together. Ask each child to point out a sentence.

3   Read through Resource sheet 7b with the children. Ask them to tick the boxes beside the correctly written sentences and then make the writing into sentences by supplying capital letters and full stops. Give reading support where necessary.

Teacher-independent activities

Choose from:

1   Have prepared sheets of paper with a few sentences from the storybook written out large, with the capital letters and full stops missing. Ask the children to mark where the capital letters and full stops should be and then check with the book to see if they were right.

2   Mount copies of Generic sheets 6 and 7 (pages 122 and 123) onto card and cut out the individual word, full stop and picture cards. Mix them up and give them to the children to make sentences with. When they have made a sentence, ask them to copy it onto paper.

3   Using the word cards only from Generic sheet 6 (page 122) ask the children to make up sentences finding objects of their own to complete the sentences. They can either write the objects' names or draw pictures of them.

Plenary session

- Write on the board 'sentence', 'capital letter' and 'full stop'. Ask for volunteers to read these and others to say what they mean.

- Ask each group to report back on what they did. Ask them to show the other children their work and explain how this helped them to learn about sentences.

- What did they learn that was new? What did they enjoy about the lesson? What was not so enjoyable?

Lesson Three

Intended learning

- To revise initial consonant clusters from the Reception year's phonics work.

- To identify initial consonant clusters in the text.

With the whole class

- Write on the board some consonant clusters, such as 'pr', 'fl', 'tr' and 'bl'. Ask the children what these say. Can they suggest some words that begin with them? For example, 'princess', 'flower', 'tree' and 'blue'.

- Remind the children of the work they did in Reception year on phonics. Can they tell you what 'phoneme', 'consonant' and 'initial consonant cluster' mean? Spend a little time reminding them what each of the terms means. Point to the examples you wrote on the board and explain that these are initial consonant clusters.

- Together agree some other examples of initial consonant clusters. Write these up and leave them on display until the lesson has finished. Can the children think of words that begin with any of these? Suggest some of your own to get them going. Write their suggestions under the appropriate cluster.

With the lower-achievers

With adult support

Choose from:

1   Together, look through *Backseat's Special Day* and ask the children to search carefully for words with initial consonant clusters and list them. They include 'sp', 'pr', 'pl', 'fr', 'tr' and 'st'. Write these at the top of a large sheet of paper. Can the children suggest other words that begin with these clusters? Together write these under the correct cluster.

2   Give each child a copy of Generic sheet 8 (page 124) and ask them to write a consonant cluster on the body of the butterfly (you might choose one for them) and examples of words beginning with that cluster on the wings. Hang these from the ceiling.

3   Give the children copies of Resource sheet 7c. They should select the appropriate consonant cluster to complete the given words. Ask them to write other words beginning with these clusters on the back of the sheet.

4   Work through the names of all the children in the group and in the class. Make a list of any that begin with consonant clusters. Challenge them to think of other names, such as Trevor and Tracey or Brenda and Bridget.

Teacher-independent activities

Choose from:

1   Prior to this activity, prepare a sheet of A4 for each child, divided into four. Head each section with an initial consonant cluster. Ask the children to go through a simple picture dictionary and write in each section the words they find beginning with the consonant clusters.

2   Using Resource sheet 7c, ask the children to select the appropriate consonant cluster to complete the given words. Then, on the back of the sheet, they could write other words that begin with the same cluster or a sentence for some of the words.

3   Use the consonant blend cards on Generic sheet 9 (page 125) to play 'Snap' or 'Pelmanism' games with.

Plenary session

■   Can the children add any new consonant clusters and words to the list on display that was used in the whole-class starter? Encourage them to come and write these up.

■   Ask the children to think of their own name and, if it begins with a consonant cluster, they could come to the front and write it on the board with the cluster in a different colour. Does anyone else in the class have the same cluster in their name?

■   Can the children tell you what 'phoneme', 'consonant' and 'initial consonant cluster' mean? Ensure they fully understand what has been taught in the lesson.

■ Put a ✔ next to the words that you think describe Backseat. You may ✔ more than one.

worried ☐   happy ☐   brave ☐

sad ☐   frightened ☐   lonely ☐

fierce ☐   funny ☐   angry ☐

Finish these sentences about Backseat.

At the beginning of the story, Backseat _____
_____

At the end of the story, Backseat _____
_____

On the back of this sheet, draw a picture of Backseat looking happy.

Put a ✔ by the correctly written sentences.

The cat jumped on the wall. ☐

my mum is very pretty. ☐

Six birds sat in a tree ☐

the boy ate ten cakes. ☐

The girl had a red hat on. ☐

A dog ran across the road ☐

✎ Put in the missing capital letters and full stops.

__en boys played football

__e go to school every day

__he man put on a big blue hat

__ou can go out to play now

| T | W | T | Y |

■ Choose the right letters to finish each word.
   Write the word under the picture.

   ___ag

_____

    ___um

_____

   ___own

_____

   ___ass

_____

Stories for story plots and themes

Overall aims

- To identify and discuss a range of story themes.
- To use capital letters for names.
- To investigate and learn spellings of words with 's' for plurals.

Featured book

Any favoured selection of fairytales.

Lesson One

Intended learning

- To use the text as a basis for discussion of the themes or morals within the stories.
- To generalise these concepts to other texts or stories.

With the whole class

- Choose a favourite story from the collection and read it with the children. If they are familiar enough with it, they could take turns to read or tell sections to the class.

- Ask the children what they think the story is about apart from the obvious storyline. Discuss the following points: the concept of good versus evil (for example, Snow White versus her stepmother/queen); good finally triumphing over evil (for example, Cinderella over the Ugly Sisters); the idea that hope is always present (for example in Hansel and Gretel); determination and persistence achieving their reward in the end (for example by the Prince in *Sleeping Beauty*); evil being always punished (for example, the Wolf in *Little Red Riding Hood* or Rumpelstiltskin).

- Ask the children to choose another story. Read it with them. Ask if there are any of the ideas in this story that they found in the first story you read together. List the common themes that appear and the names of the stories that feature these. These should include 'good and evil', 'good wins', 'evil fails' and 'bravery'. Add to the list as more stories are read and discussed.

With the lower-achievers

With adult support

Choose from:

1. Choose another fairytale and share it with the children, encouraging them to do the actual reading. Talk about the moral and thematic ideas of the story and compare it with the discussion during the whole-class session. Use the text and the illustrations to reinforce any points that are not clear to them.

2. Tell the children they are going to act out the story. Ask them which roles they want to play and why. Can they explain the difference between how they will act if they are good or if they are evil? Which do they prefer? Why? Act out the story. (This can be done away from the main classroom.)

3. Give the children copies of Resource sheet 8a and ask them to match the pictures of fairytales to the statements they think are true. Explain that more than one story could be matched to one statement. Give support where necessary. Discuss their answers to the last question.

4. Let the group make a 'good/evil' chart by dividing a large sheet of paper into two and sticking in the relevant places the characters from Generic sheet 10 (page 126).

Teacher-independent activities

Choose from:

1. Ask the children to choose another favourite fairy tale and read it together in pairs. They should discuss the thematic ideas already talked about in the whole-class session. Ask them to add to the 'theme' list in the correct places the name of the new story they read .

2. Ask the children to use puppets to tell a chosen fairytale, bringing out the idea, for example, of the good and evil elements. (If puppets aren't available, simple finger-covers, for example made from paper or cut-up rubber gloves, illustrated as each character can be made.) Tell them they are going to give a performance of their puppet-show in the plenary session.

3. Enlarge the statements from Resource sheet 8a and stick each onto a separate sheet of paper. Ask the children to work in pairs and write on

each sheet the titles of all the fairytales they know which match each statement.

4 Let the group make a 'good/evil' chart by dividing a large sheet of paper into two and sticking in the relevant places the characters from Generic sheet 10 (page 126).

Plenary session

■ Look again at the list of themes that you started in the whole-class session. Discuss together any additions. Which titles have been added? Why? Have any new themes been added? If so, what tales can be put into the new theme sections?

■ Ask the children who used puppets to give a performance of their play. Ask the whole class what themes or ideas came out of the performance. Can the children suggest other fairy tales that would make good puppet plays?

■ Challenge the children to read other stories (not necessarily fairytales) bearing in mind the ideas and themes discussed in the lesson. Keep the list on the wall and encourage them to add to it over time.

Lesson Two

Intended learning

■ To use capital letters for names.

■ To explore a variety of texts for the use of capital letters for names.

With the whole class

■ Before starting the lesson, write on the board several of the children's names in lower case letters. Make sure the children have their own names on cards ready to look at. Can those whose names are on the board tell you what's wrong? Can the children as a whole identify your 'mistake'?

■ Ask for volunteers (not the children whose names have been written) to come and write the names again but correctly. Can the children tell the difference?

■ Do they use the term 'capital letters'? If not, remind them of it. Ask them where they have heard of it before. (At the beginning of sentences.) Explain that it is also used for people's names.

■ Ask them to look at their name cards. What do they notice about the first letter of both their first and family names?

■ Can they tell you where else they might see written names? (Books, magazines, papers, the class register, CDs, video covers, advertisements and so on.) Make a list of the children's suggestions and leave it displayed for reference or to be added to.

With the lower-achievers

With adult support

Choose from:

1 Ensure that the children can see an alphabet with upper case letters. Write on the board each child's first name minus the initial letter. Ask the group what each name begins with and then ask a volunteer (not the child whose name it is) to write the missing letter.

2 Using Resource sheet 8b, ask the children to change or complete the names with capital letters, as required. Give reading support where necessary.

3 Select a variety of texts that have names in them. For example, some of the fairytales in the list drawn up in the whole-class session. Look through these together with the children. Can they identify names in the text? Do the names have capital letters? Ask them to identify names on title pages, on doors, on personal property? Do these names always start with a capital letter?

4 Play 'Hangman' using the children's names. Always write the initial letter as a capital, but ensure the rest of the name is written in lower case to illustrate the point.

Teacher-independent activities

Choose from:

1   Ask the children to draw a picture of all the members of their family. They should then write on the bottom of the sheet the names of each family member. Remind them to use capital letters. Accept that there may well be some spelling mistakes but the first letter of each name should be a capital.

2   Ask the children to look through the chosen fairytale book for some names. Ask them to make two lists, one of male and one of female names that they come across. Remind them to write these with capital initial letters.

3   Prepare sheets of A4 headed with the last names from a set of 'Happy Family' cards (one family name per sheet). Give each child a sheet and ask them to find the appropriate set of cards. Ask them to write on the sheet all the names of the family members from their set. They could then draw portraits of the 'Happy Family'.

4   Give the children a picture of a baby or a pet. Ask them to work in pairs to make a list of suitable names. Alternatively it could be a competition to guess the name which you have previously sealed in an envelope. You could announce the name in the plenary session.

Plenary session

■   Ask the children what they have learned about writing names. If necessary, remind them about the use of capital letters.

■   Write a few names on the board in lower case letters and ask for volunteers to change these.

■   Ask the groups who completed the resource sheets or 'Happy Family' sheets to share with the class what they did.

■   Did the class understand everything they were told about using capital letters for names? Is there anything they found difficult?

■   Reveal the name from the guessing game. Who was the closest?

Lesson Three

Intended learning

■   To investigate and learn spellings of words with 's' for plurals.

■   To explore a variety of texts for the use of 's' for plurals.

With the whole class

■   Write on the board several regular words in the singular. For example, 'dog', 'cake', 'house', 'cup', 'book' and so on. Read them with the children. Then point to each word in turn and ask, *"What would I write if I had two of these?"* If necessary, give one or two examples to show the children what you want.

■   Write the plurals under the singular words as they are offered by the children. What do they notice about the words now? Can any of them come and point out the difference? When saying the plurals, emphasise the 's' of each word. Highlight the 's' with a different colour or a circle.

■   Can the children give you examples of plurals that are written on captions and labels around the classroom? Write these on the board. Explain that 's' is usually added to a word to make it into the plural.

■   Read out some passages from the chosen fairytale book. Can the children identify any plural words? Make a list of the words they discover, which can be added to later.

■   Can the children tell you what word is used when talking of more than one? Write 'plural' on the board and read it to them. Explain that this is the correct term and they should use it from now on. (Don't deal with irregular plurals at this stage.)

With the lower-achievers

With adult support

Choose from:

1   Use a set of photograph noun cards such as those produced by LDA (Learning Development Aids). Make sure they are not nouns that have irregular plurals. Show each card to the children and say *"Tell me what the plural is."* Make sure they say the word with 's'. Write the singular on the board and as you write say *"This is the singular. Can you turn it into a plural?"* Together agree a sentence for the words to go into and write it up for the children to read together.

2   Using Resource sheet 8c, ask the children to make the given singular words into plurals and then complete the sentences by choosing the correct plural word. Ask them to write some plural words they can see in the classroom.

3   Play 'Pelmanism' but let the child keep their pair only after they have named the pictures correctly in the plural.

Teacher-independent activities

Choose from:

1   Ask the children to make a collection of small items in duplicate or triplicate. (Plastic sorting sets of animals, shapes and so on can be used.) Ask them to write labels for these in both the singular and the plural. Make a table display. For example, the 'dog' label would be in front of the single dog, while 'dogs' would be in front of the group of two or three dogs. The whole display should consist of four or five categories of items.

2   Let the children complete Resource sheet 8c.

3   Ask the children to draw pictures of everything that we wear in plurals. For example, shoes, gloves, wellingtons, socks, trainers, earrings and so on. Ask them to write the names of their pictures, remembering to put them into the plural.

Plenary session

■   Before bringing the class together again, collect several items to show the children. For example, a book, a pencil, a hat, a doll, a flower and so on. Hold up each item and ask what its plural is. Ask for volunteers to write the word on the board. Do they remember the 's'?

■   Ask each group to report back to the whole class what they did. Ask the group that made the table display to explain to the others what they did, how and why.

■   Has everybody understood that they should use 's' when talking or writing about plurals? What did they like about the lesson? What did they find difficult?

Name _____

■ Read these sentences. Match them to the fairytale pictures. You might match them more than once.

There is a good person and a bad person in the story.

The bad person is punished in the end.

The people in the story never give up and they win in the end.

The good person has a happy ending in the story.

■ Do you like happy endings? Put a ✔

Yes ☐   No ☐

■ Write your name here. Don't forget the capital letters.

■ Write the names of two of your friends.

■ Write these names. Use capital letters to start them.

dick whittington   rumpelstiltskin

_____   _____

■ Write the correct capital letters to complete the names.

✏ _ a n s e l   _ a c k   _ n o w   W h i t e

_ r e t e l   _ i n d e r e l l a

[G]   [H]   [S]   [J]   [C]

■ Read these words. Now write them in the plural.

dog   ball   girl   boy

 _____   _____   _____   _____

■ Complete these sentences by choosing a word.

Five _____ were playing in the park. < girl / girls

My brother has lots of _____. < toys / toy

The dog chased six _____ . < rabbits / rabbit

The _____ sang to each other. < bird / birds

 Write some plural words of your own.

_____

_____

Poems with actions

Overall aims

- To explore action poems and learn how to recite them, with actions.

- To use the studied action poems as a basis for own work.

- To extend the analysis of action poems by adding new lines and/or actions.

Featured book

First Verses compiled by John Foster

Lesson One

Chosen poem

'Three Purple Elephants' by Joan Poulson
(See page 68)

Intended learning

- To explore action poems and learn how to recite them, with actions.

- To use the studied action poems as a basis for own work.

With the whole class

- Enlarge two copies of 'Three Purple Elephants'. Tell the children that they are going to learn some poetry that they can perform actions to. Explain that not all poetry is just to sit and listen to!

- Read the poem with the children. Point to the text during reading. Ask the children what actions could be done in this poem. How do they know? Encourage them to use the text to decide the actions they are going to adopt.

- Can the children invent some new lines for the poem? Discuss with them the possibility of other animals in other colours that might join those in the poem. For example, green monkeys, an orange orang-utan or a black and white dog. What actions might the new animals

perform? Can the children invent hand actions to show these? Write the new lines on the second enlarged copy of the poem.

- Practise the words of the verses of the original poem until the children are able to recite them. Encourage them to do the actions at the right places.

With the lower-achievers

With adult support

Choose from:

(Some of this work may need to be done away from the main classroom.)

1   Look at the enlarged copy of the original version of 'Three Purple Elephants'. Read the first verse, pointing to the text during reading. Encourage the children to join in. Ask them to perform the actions chosen for the poem during the whole-class session.

2   Draw symbols for the actions on the enlarged copy of the poem. Ask the children to practise the actions to give a class performance. Can they also learn the new lines and actions that they made up? If so, use the enlarged copy that has these written on it.

3   Using Resource sheet 9a, ask the children to match the pictures of the children to the action words. Help them to write a sentence for each one.

Teacher-independent activities

Choose from:

1   Enlarge and cut out the action words from Resource sheet 9a. Ask the children to draw animals that would do the actions. For example, 'wave' could be for an elephant waving its trunk or 'hop' could be for a rabbit.

2   Ask the children to look through a set of verb cards (such as those produced by LDA) and choose two or three that could be used as new actions for the poem. (If necessary, limit the set of cards to just a few to look through, rather than giving them the whole box.)

3   Ask the children to look through other poetry or nursery rhyme anthologies to find action poems. They should share these, reading them

and doing the actions. Ask them to choose one or two to share at the plenary session.

4   Using Resource sheet 9a, ask the children to match the pictures of the children to the action words. Can they write a sentence for each one?

Plenary session

■   Look again at the second enlarged copy of 'Three Purple Elephants' which has the new lines. Challenge the children to recite the poem, do the actions and continue with the new lines.

■   Ask the children who looked through other anthologies to share with the class one or two of the poems they found. Can they recite these and do the actions?

■   Do the children still think poetry is just for listening to? Do they enjoy poetry with actions? Can they think of some actions to go with a favourite nursery rhyme such as 'Jack and Jill'?

Lesson Two

Chosen poem

'The Band' – traditional (See page 69)

Intended learning

■   To explore action poems and learn how to recite them, with actions.

■   To extend the analysis of action poems by adding new lines and/or actions.

With the whole class

■   Enlarge a copy of 'The Band'. Remind the children of the work already covered on action poems. Tell them they are going to look at another action poem.

■   Read 'The Band' with the children, pointing to the text during reading. Ask them what the poem is about. If possible, look at a poster of an orchestra or band and discuss what each instrument in the poem looks and sounds like.

■   Discuss what actions would be appropriate for the instrument in each verse. Practise the words of the first verse until the children are able to recite it. Encourage them to do the actions at the right places.

■   Can the children name any other musical instruments for the poem? What actions would they have to perform to show these instruments? What words would they use to write a new verse for them? For example, if they named a guitar, they might suggest 'twang' as the word for line three of the new verse. Write the new verse(s) on the enlarged copy.

With the lower-achievers

With adult support

Choose from:

(Some of this work may have to be done away from the main classroom.)

1   Listen to a tape of musical instruments. Discuss what each one featured in the poem sounds like. Look again at pictures of an orchestra or band. If possible have some examples of real instruments for the children to examine and explore. Together with the children make labels for each instrument and put these on display, either on the poster or next to the real instrument.

2   Share the poem again with the children, encouraging them to recite the first verse unaided. Work on the following verses, practising the agreed actions for each one. Can they also learn the new verse(s) written in the whole-class session?

3   Encourage the children to choose one or two other instruments and add new lines to the poem. Write these on Resource sheet 9b. Decide on actions to go with the new lines. Learn the new lines and practise the actions.

Teacher-independent activities

Choose from:

1   Ask the children to copy out their favourite verse of 'The Band'. Ask them to illustrate it. Challenge them to work in pairs to write a new verse.

2   Give the children copies of Resource sheet 9c and ask them to write words around the pictures that describe the sound each one makes.

3   Provide each child with an enlarged copy of the poem. Using Resource sheet 9c, ask them to cut out the pictures and names of the musical instruments and stick them in the appropriate places on the enlarged poem. Ask them to write a word for the sound each instrument makes.

4   Using Resource sheet 9b, ask the children to write the new lines made up in the whole-class session. Let them refer to the enlarged copy if necessary.

Plenary session

■   Ask one child from each group to tell the others what they did. Encourage the children with resource sheets or books to show the class their writing and drawings.

■   If the real instruments are available, practise reciting the poem using the instruments at the appropriate places. The children without instruments can do the agreed actions. (If possible give a performance at school assembly. Be prepared for a lot of noise!)

■   Encourage the children to share with everybody how they feel about action poems. Ensure that each opinion is respected and valued. It is especially important to encourage those children who did not enjoy the sessions to express their opinions and feel these are as valid as those of the other children.

Three purple elephants

There were three purple elephants,
A little pink mouse,
A black and white panda,
A yellow wooden house.

I opened the door
Of my yellow wooden house,
Said, Come inside, panda.
Come inside, mouse.

The three purple elephants said,
What about us?
I'm sorry but you'll have to get
The Number Five bus.

Joan Poulson

The band

We can play on the big bass drum,
And this is the music to it:
Boom – boom – boom goes the big bass drum,
And that's the way we do it!

We can play on the violin,
And this is the music to it:
Zing – zing – zing goes the violin,
And that's the way we do it!

We can play on the saxophone,
And this is the music to it:
Soo – soo – soo goes the saxophone,
And that's the way we do it!

We can play on the tambourine,
And this is the music to it:
Tink – tink – tink goes the tambourine,
And that's the way we do it!

Traditional

■ Match the pictures to the action words.

clap

jump

wave

sing

hop

run

Name _____

■ Write the new lines of The Band here.

We can play on the _____

And this is the music to it:

_____ goes the _____

And that's the way we do it!

· ·

We can play on the _____

And this is the music to it:

_____ goes the _____

And that's the way we do it!

· ·

We can play on the _____

And this is the music to it:

_____ goes the _____

And that's the way we do it!

■ Cut out the pictures and stick them on the large poem in the right places.

violin

tambourine

big bass drum

saxophone

Poems for learning and reciting

Overall aims

- To explore several poems that are familiar but with a new slant.
- To use these poems as a basis for learning and reciting poetry.
- To use the poems as a basis for developing own work and reciting it.

Featured book

Nonsense Counting Rhymes by Kaye Umansky

Lesson One

Chosen poems

'Supper time' and 'Sing a song of sixpence' by Kaye Umansky (See page 76)

Intended learning

- To explore several poems that are familiar but with a new slant.
- To use these poems as a basis for learning and reciting poetry.

With the whole class

- Enlarge copies of 'Supper time' and 'Sing a song of sixpence'. Tell the children that they are going to learn some nursery rhymes, but nursery rhymes with a difference.
- Read 'Supper time' with them, pointing to the text and letting them join in. Ask them what they notice about the rhyme. Have they heard of something like this before? Agree what it is.
- Allocate a line of the poem to five of the children. (Be very sensitive to cultural and social practices when doing this.) Ask each child to say their line in turn so that they recite the whole rhyme between them. (This may need to be done over more than one session.)
- Read 'Sing a song of sixpence' with the children. Pause at the end of each line before saying the alternative words. Encourage them to

enjoy this variation on the nursery rhyme. Again, give different children a line each to recite. (This may need to be done over more than one session.)

With the lower-achievers

With adult support

Choose from:

1 Revisit 'Supper time' and 'Sing a song of sixpence' with the children. Ask them whether they like these poems. Can they say why or why not?

2 Give the children copies of Resource sheet 10a. Ask them to write the first line of 'Supper time' using the enlarged copies for reference. Then ask them to write how the little pig laid the table, using the given words to help if they wish. Give support where necessary.

3 As in the whole-class session, allocate the lines of the poems to individual children. If necessary, split a line between them, allocating one or more words according to ability. Practise reciting the poems (this can be done away from the main classroom if necessary) to give a performance for the class.

4 Using Resource sheet 10b, ask the children to rewrite 'Supper time' using the given words to help them. Ask them to complete the sentence at the bottom of the sheet. Give reading support where necessary.

Teacher-independent activities

Choose from:

1 Ask the children to draw pictures to illustrate 'Supper time' and/or 'Sing a song of sixpence'. They might be able to write one or two words as captions to go with the pictures.

2 Ask the children to look through other nursery rhyme or poetry books from the classroom library. Ask them to choose one rhyme and see if they can alter one or two words to make a new version. According to ability, they might replace some of the words with pictures.

3 Give the children copies of Resource sheet 10b. They are asked to rewrite 'Supper time' using the given words to help them. Ask them to

complete the sentence at the bottom of the sheet.

4   Ask the children to role-play one of the rhymes. Tell them they will have the opportunity to give a performance at the plenary session if they wish to.

Plenary session

■   Ask for volunteers from the children who have written new versions or additional verses to share their work with the whole class.

■   Ask the children whether they enjoyed working with these rhymes. Can they say why? Or why not? Do they prefer the original versions to the new ones? Why or why not? Encourage them to develop an opinion and express it with confidence.

■   Ask the children who role-played one of the rhymes to give a performance for the class.

Lesson Two

Chosen poems

'Eight cakes' and 'One, two, three, four, five' by Kaye Umansky (See page 77)

Intended learning

■   To explore several poems that are familiar but with a new slant.

■   To use the poems as a basis for developing own work and reciting it.

With the whole class

■   Enlarge 'One, two, three, four, five' and 'Eight cakes'. Tell the children they are going to learn some more rhymes. Read 'One, two, three, four, five' with them, pointing to the text during reading. Pause before the ends of the lines allowing the children to either read the words or offer the endings themselves. What does the poem remind them of? Can they

recite the original to you? Do they like this new version? Why does the poet say 'Don't think I'll do that again!'?

■   Ask the children to think of new versions of lines two and four. Recite the poems so that you say line one, a child offers a 'new' line two, you read line three and another child suggests line four. They should all be able to come up with an alternative for 'Once I caught a ?? alive' but might have problems with the last line, so you could revert to the original. Write the new poem the children thought of on a large sheet of paper.

■   Read 'Eight cakes' to the children pointing to the text during reading. Again, allocate lines to individual children to practise reciting. (This may need to be done over more than one session.)

■   Tell the children they are going to do some of their own poetry composition in groups.

With the lower-achievers

With adult support

Choose from:

1   Revisit 'One, two, three, four, five' and 'Eight cakes'. Ask the children if they like these poems. Can they say why or why not? Discuss how they have been taken from a nursery rhyme they know and that some words have been changed. Remind them of the original version. Read the second line of 'One, two, three, four, five'. Can the children say which word has changed? Could they think of another word to put in place of that and change the rhyme again?

2   Working closely with the children, ask them to choose a nursery rhyme that they would like to rewrite. Encourage them to offer alternative words. Tell them that their new words don't have to rhyme, but the poem must make sense. Give them some examples:

'Little Jack Horner sat in a corner,

Eating a bag of sweets;

He put in his thumb and pulled out a toffee,

And said, "I like chocolate more!"'

Write the children's new nursery rhyme on a large sheet of paper.

3   Using Resource sheet 10c, read the poem with the children. Ask them what a hive is and also why the writer will never put their nose into another hive again. Ask them to draw a picture to go with the poem and to then complete the new poem at the bottom of the sheet, using the words provided to help them.

Teacher-independent activities

Choose from:

1   Give the children a line each to learn from either of the poems and ask them to practise it so that they can recite it to the class in the plenary session. The group should help any of those who are struggling.

2   Enlarge and cut out the poem on Resource sheet 10b. Then cut it into the two-line sections. Give the children a section each (or each pair of children a section each) and ask them to think of a final word for their own section. They should then get back together and read the poem a section at a time, in the right order with the new words. They could come up with several versions for the plenary session.

3   Ask the children to write out their two favourite lines from 'Eight cakes' or 'One, two, three, four, five'. They could then illustrate the rhyme.

4   Ask the children to complete Resource sheet 10c on their own, according to ability.

Plenary session

■   Pin up the enlarged version of 'One, two, three, four, five' beside the sheet of paper with the children's own version written on it. Ask the children to tell you how the two versions differ. Ask how both versions differ from the traditional original. Which of the three versions do they prefer and why?

■   Ask those children who looked for new versions of traditional rhymes to share their favourites with the class. Read aloud some of the rhymes they chose.

■   Ask the children whether they found these lessons difficult. Did they enjoy the work? Do they feel differently about poetry now? Can they tell you how and why?

Supper time

This little pig laid the table,
This little pig stirred the pot,
This little pig laid the fire,
This little pig made it hot.
This little pig cried, 'Wee wee! Stew for tea!'
And ate the lot!

Kaye Umansky

Sing a song of sixpence

Sing a song of sixpence,
A pocket full of cheese,
Four and twenty monkeys
Swinging in the trees.
They picked all the bananas
And dropped them on my head.
I had to call the monkey king
Who sent them off to bed.

Kaye Umansky

Eight cakes

Two, four, six, eight!
Count the cakes the giant ate.
Stop him quick! He'll eat the plate!
Oh dear. Too late.

Kaye Umansky

One, two, three, four, five

One, two, three, four, five,
Once I caught a shark alive,
Six, seven, eight, nine, ten.
Don't think I'll do that again!

Kaye Umansky

■ Write the first line from 'Supper Time'.

_____

■ How do you think the little pig laid the table? Use the words to help you.

First he_____

_____

Then he _____

_____

Next he_____

_____

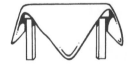

■ Can you write a new poem like 'Supper time'?
Use the words below to help you.

This little pig made the _____

This little pig stirred the pot,

This little pig cooked the _____

This little pig made a lot,

This little pig cried, 'Wee wee,

_____ for tea!'

■ Finish the sentence.
My favourite poem is _____ .

■ Read this poem.

One, two, three, four, five,

Put my nose into a hive,

Six, seven, eight, nine, ten,

Learnt my lesson – never again!

■ Write a new poem using the words
to help you.

One, two, three, four, five,

Once I caught a _____ alive,

Six, seven, eight, nine, ten,

Think I'll _____ again.

| dragon | | spider |

| run away | | lion |

| throw it back | | catch a fish |

Stories with unfamiliar storylines

Overall aims

■ To use the title page, illustrations and blurb of a book to predict the content of an unfamiliar story.

■ To be aware of word order by reordering sentences to make grammatical sense.

■ To investigate and learn spellings with 'ed' for the past tense.

Featured book

Whiff or How the Beautiful Big Fat Smelly Baby Found a Friend by Ian Whybrow and Russell Ayto

Story synopsis

Whiff is an extremely smelly baby warthog who is the pride and joy of his mum and dad. They want Whiff to be happy and make friends. He goes to play with the baby crocodile and all goes well until the flies come down, attracted by Whiff's smell. The crocodile and Whiff thrash around and wreck the house. Whiff is sent home in disgrace. The same thing happens when he goes to tea with the baby monkeys. All ends well, however, when he goes to play with Baby Littlebird, who happily gobbles up all the flies. Whiff becomes a popular friend of the Littlebird household, who are delighted with the dietary spin-off that the friendship brings.

Lesson One
. . . .

Intended learning

■ To focus on the title page, illustrations and blurb of the featured book in order to predict what the story might be about.

■ To understand that the title pages, illustrations and blurbs of all books give valuable information about the book.

With the whole class

■ Show the cover of the book to the children. Do they know what the animal is? Have they heard of a warthog? Where? Point to the bird. Have they seen one like this? Can they tell you what

the insects are? And why they are swarming around Whiff?

■ Can the children guess what this story might be about judging from the cover illustration? Write their suggestions on the board to refer back to after the story has been explored.

■ Read the blurb on the back cover, and discuss with the children the hints it gives about the story. It mentions that Whiff is always getting into trouble, and that he has problems in making friends. Can they suggest a reason for this? The blurb explains that all ends well for Whiff. Can the children guess why? Again, write their ideas on the board for later reference.

■ Spend time looking at some of the illustrations in the book. (At this stage don't read the text.) Discuss the pictures with the children. Encourage them to make suggestions about the story, using only the illustrations as a basis.

■ Read the story to the children, letting them see the text and the illustrations. Keep stopping at strategic points in the story (for example, when the flies descend, after the house has been wrecked and so on) and ask what they think will happen next.

■ When you have finished, ask them if the story had turned out the way they expected. Did the blurb give a good idea of the story? Did the pictures help them to decide what was going to happen in the story? Explain to the children that they can discover what is in any book by looking at the cover, the illustrations and the blurb.

■ Look at one or two other (familiar) books and discuss how the blurb and illustrations help to show what the story is about.

With the lower-achievers

With adult support

Choose from:

1 Look again at the blurb on the back cover of *Whiff*. Read it with the children. Do they think it is a good description of what the story is about? Can they tell you why they think it is or isn't? Discuss again the cover illustration.

2 Choose two more books that the children are unfamiliar with. Focus on the covers, 'blurbs' and illustrations. Together with the children, discuss the possible contents of each book. Help them to write some sentences for each book, predicting its storyline. (After the books are read, encourage them to read their predictions and judge how accurate they were.)

3 Ask the children to each name a favourite story. Discuss together what they might put in the blurb for that book. Help them to write it out.

4 Give the children copies of Resource sheet 11a. Give support with reading where necessary.

Teacher-independent activities

Choose from:

1 Have ready some photocopies of covers and blurbs from books in the classroom. Ask the children to work in pairs to match the blurbs to the correct covers. They could then find the books to check if they were right.

2 Ask the children to design covers for two of their favourite fairy stories. They could then write a 'blurb' for each story. Make a classroom 'Blurb book' that can be added to over time.

3 Ask the children to complete Resource sheet 11a. They could find the original books and compare their blurbs with those on the sheet.

4 Ask the children to work in pairs and read the blurbs of two unfamiliar stories. Ask them to record into a tape recorder what they think the stories might be about. (After they have read the books, they can see how accurate their predictions were. Did they find the blurbs useful? And accurate?)

Plenary session

■ Read together the lists of suggestions about *Whiff* that were written (before reading the book) in the whole–class session. Did the children manage to predict the storyline? Ask them whether they think the blurb and the illustrations in *Whiff* helped them to guess what the story was going to be about.

■ Did any of the children come across unfamiliar stories during their group work? Were they

enticed to read the stories from the blurbs? Were the illustrations helpful? Can the children tell you how they would become interested in an unfamiliar book? Encourage them to use blurbs, illustrations and covers for any new book they come across.

■ Ask for volunteers to talk about a new book they discovered. Can they share with the others how the blurb and the illustrations made them want to read the book? Encourage them to explain what they found interesting about the artwork.

Lesson Two

Intended learning

■ To be aware of word order by reordering sentences to make grammatical sense.

■ To use a variety of texts to explore the order of sentences that make sense.

With the whole class

■ Write on the board a few simple and familiar sentences, out of word order. For example, 'Humpty wall on sat a Dumpty' or 'clock The up ran mouse the'. Can any of the children read these? Can they tell you the correct word order? Ask for volunteers to write the suggestions under each sentence. Do they make sense? Work with these sentences until the children have them in the right order.

■ Now write a few unfamiliar sentences, out of order. For example, 'wall boy the jumped The over' or 'dog six had My pups'. Ask the children to read these as they are written. Challenge them to find the correct order. Can they tell you how they decided this?

■ Discuss some of the following points. Did they use the word with the capital letter as the first word? Did they put a noun next? What type of word followed that? ('Verb' or 'doing word'.) Did they use another noun then? Did they check whether the two nouns were in the right place to make sense?

With the lower-achievers

With adult support

Choose from:

1 Give the children copies of Resource sheet 11b. Give support where necessary. If appropriate, work with the sentences on the board first.

2 Choose two or three sentences from *Whiff* and write them on the board, out of order. Read them together with the children. Can they tell you what's wrong? Can they put the sentences back into order? Write out the correct order and challenge the children to read them. Or can they write the correct order on the board themselves?

3 Prior to this activity enlarge Resource sheet 11b, stick it onto card and cut out the individual words of each sentence. Play a game with the children where they have to sort the cards into sentences that make sense. How many different sentences can they make? At the end, scribe the group's sentences.

4 Choose two or three sentences from a familiar book and write them on the board with the words out of order. Can the children read them to you as they are? Can they tell you the correct order? Challenge them to write the correct order by themselves.

Teacher-independent activities

Choose from:

1 Enlarge Resource sheet 11b, stick it onto card and cut out the individual words. Mix up all the words and ask the children to play a game where they have to choose any words they wish from all the cards, to make sentences. Challenge them to make funny sentences, but remind them that these have to make sense by being in the right order.

2 Make some flash cards using high frequency words. Put these into a 'feely bag'. You will also need tokens or tiddlywinks. The children can play a game in pairs, where they take two words from the bag, read them aloud and then (verbally) make up a sentence including the words. The other children in the group must agree whether it makes sense. If it does, the child takes a token or tiddlywink; the winner has the most after a set time.

3 Organise the children into pairs and give them a set of noun pictures. They choose two pictures and make a sensible sentence for them. For example, pictures of a boy and a dog could lead to 'The boy played with his dog'. They should record their sentences into a cassette recorder.

4 Let the children complete Resource sheet 11b.

Plenary session

■ Ask the children who completed Resource sheet 11b to explain what they did and why. Can any of them tell you why word order is important? Ask the class what would happen if all our books were written in any order.

■ Ask the children who recorded sentences into the cassette recorder to show the picture cards to the class and play their recordings.

■ Write another sentence on the board with the words mixed up. Ask the children to say what the correct order is.

Lesson Three

Intended learning

■ To understand the term 'past tense'.

■ To investigate and learn spellings with 'ed' for the past tense.

■ To explore a variety of texts for words ending with 'ed' (past tense).

With the whole class

■ Prior to the lesson, write on the board a few regular past tense words such as 'called', 'played', 'walked' and 'jumped'.

■ Ask the children to look at all the words you have written. Read them together. What do they notice about them? Can they tell you why the words end in 'ed'? Ask for volunteers to come and highlight with a different colour the 'ed' of each word.

- Explain that when we are writing about something that has already happened, we call it the past tense. (Ask the children to tell you what 'verbs' are.) Look again at the words on the board and focus on the highlighted 'ed' of each word. Together with the children, think of sentences using these 'ed' words.

- Write on the board the following words: 'laugh', 'help', 'want', 'push' and 'pull'. Ask the children to put these into the past tense. Can they tell you how? Encourage different children to add 'ed' themselves to a word.

With the lower-achievers

With adult support

Choose from:

1   Either on a large sheet of paper or on the board, write out the following verbs: 'call', 'help', 'jump', 'laugh', 'pull', 'push' and 'want'. Ask the children to put the words into the past tense. Work closely with them to help them to learn the words. You could use the 'Look, say, cover, write, check' method.

2   Ask the children to complete Resource sheet 11c. Give help where necessary.

3   Challenge the children to think of as many examples as they can of regular verbs in the past tense. List their suggestions – each child could write their examples on a large 'communal' sheet of paper. Give each child a different coloured pen for their own suggestions.

Teacher-independent activities

Choose from:

1   Challenge the children to work in pairs to learn the words written on the board in the whole-class session. They should take each word individually, look at it, say each letter, cover the word, say the letters again, write the word and then check it against the model. Can they learn each word in fewer than five attempts? Fewer than three?

2   Ask the children to complete Resource sheet 11c independently.

3   Ask them to look through *Whiff* for some examples of regular past tenses and list them.

4   Give the children some photograph verb cards (make sure they are regular verb pictures) or a copy of Generic sheet 11 (page 127), cut up into cards and mounted. They should place the cards face down on the table. Each child in the group turns over one card and has to say the verb in the past tense to the others. If they agree it is correct, the child may keep the card. The winner has the highest number of cards.

Plenary session

(Before the plenary session, put on the board the wordsearch from Resource sheet 11c.)

- Can the children tell you what 'past tense' means? Ask them how we would write a verb in the past tense. Challenge volunteers to come and write on the board the 'ed' words they have learned. (Unaided!)

- Challenge volunteers to find the 'ed' words in the wordsearch.

- Ask a spokesperson from each group to tell the class what they did during their group activities.

- Make sure everybody has understood what the lesson was about. Ask *"Did anybody have any difficulties with this work?"*

■ Match the blurbs to the book covers.

The wicked fairy says the princess will die. But the princess only sleeps for a long time...

The girl has to do all the dirty jobs. But she goes to the party in a magic carriage. She meets the prince...

The girl goes into a house and eats some of the porridge. She sits on a chair and breaks it. She sleeps in a little bed...

The boy grows a plant that goes up to the sky. He climbs up and takes the giant's gold. He kills the giant...

■ Write the sentences in the correct order.

| jumped | The | wall | the | over | cat |

_____

| ate | bars | six | of | chocolate | Mum |

_____

| brother | mouse | pet | My | has | a |

_____

| after | rabbit | the | The | ran | dog |

_____

| to | fish | catch | a | wanted | Dad |

_____

Name _____

■ Write these words in the past tense.

call   help   jump   pull   want

_____   _____   _____   ____   _____

■ Now find these words in the wordsearch.

c	p	u	s	h	e	d	c
w	u	h	j	e	c	a	a
a	l	a	u	g	h	e	d
n	l	j	m	h	e	l	p
t	e	u	p	u	l	a	u
e	d	d	e	e	p	u	l
d	e	c	d	p	e	g	a
c	a	l	l	e	d	h	u

pushed

jumped

wanted

pulled

called

laughed

■ Write some more words that end in 'ed'.

_____   _____   _____

■ Put them into sentences.

_____

_____

_____

Stories with familiar settings

Overall aims

- To explore stories that reflect familiar settings and situations.
- To understand that personal titles begin with a capital letter.
- To focus on and learn some of the high frequency words.

Featured book

Titch by Pat Hutchins

Story synopsis

Titch is the youngest and the smallest in his family. All the bigger and better things seem to be owned by his older brother and sister. Except for the tiny seed which Titch has and which he plants in his sister's large pot, in soil put in by his brother, using a big spade. Titch's tiny seed grows to a huge plant. The book illustrates the difficulties of being the youngest and smallest, but also shows that this state does not last forever.

Lesson One

Intended learning

- To explore stories that reflect familiar settings and situations.
- To work with the chosen text and show how being the smallest or youngest in a family can be difficult.
- To discuss other familiar situations, for example, the arrival of a new baby, finding schoolwork difficult or bullying.

With the whole class

- Show the cover to the children and ask what the book's title is. If they don't know and can't read it, tell them it is called *Titch*. Ask them what 'titch' means. Have they heard of it before? Agree that it means 'small'. Would they like this nickname? Discuss one or two other nicknames (being careful not to use any that

might hurt feelings). What nickname would they like to have?

- Read the story to the children. Ask them to describe what Titch's problem is and how they know. Draw attention to Titch's facial expressions. What do they think Titch is feeling in each picture? Do any of them feel unhappy because they are the youngest or the smallest in their family?

- Can the children name other situations that may be difficult for them? If necessary, give them one or two examples to start off, such as going into hospital, bullying or a new baby. Write on the board the ideas that they suggest. Explore with the class how each of these situations might make them feel. Encourage them to use words to describe their emotions, such as 'unhappy', 'angry', 'jealous' and 'sad'. Leave the words on the board for reference.

With the lower-achievers

With adult support

Choose from:

1   Reread the story to the group. Ask if they would feel like Titch. Do they think Titch was happy in the end? How did he achieve this? Ask the children to role-play the story. Encourage them to think about the feelings of their role-character. Ask them to practise their play to give a class performance.

2   Look at other books with familiar settings, such as *Dogger* by Shirley Hughes, *Where's my Mum?* by Leon Rosselson and *Amazing Grace* by Mary Hoffman. Discuss each situation and how it affects the child in the book. Can the children tell you how they would feel if they were in that situation?

3   Give the children copies of Resource sheet 12a to complete. Give support if necessary.

4   Discuss with the children what other familiar situations might make them unhappy. Refer to the list drawn up in the whole-class session. Can they add to this? Have any of the children experienced any of the situations? How did they feel about it? (Be extremely sensitive during this discussion. Don't attempt to force reluctant children to share their experiences. Be aware

also of comments that may be an indication of a situation that needs to be looked into.)

Teacher-independent activities

Choose from:

1   Prepare a cassette on which are recorded the emotion words from the whole-class session, such as 'unhappy', 'angry', 'jealous' and 'sad'. (Make sure you leave a gap of three or four seconds between each word to allow the children to switch the player on and off.) Ask the children to work in pairs and decide on situations that might result in the emotions on the cassette. They should draw a picture to illustrate each. If possible they should write some of the emotion words under their pictures. (Remind them that the words are on the board.)

2   Ask the children to work in pairs to look at one or two of the other books dealing with a familiar situation. Provide pictures of people whose faces are showing different emotions (or use Generic sheet 1, page 117). The children should discuss the stories and agree which of the faces in the pictures match the feelings of the main characters.

3   Ask the children to think about a situation they have experienced, such as going to hospital or losing a grandparent. Ask them to draw a picture about it and write some words about it underneath.

4   Ask the children to complete Resource sheet 12a. Give reading support beforehand if necessary.

Plenary session

■   Ask the group that did the role-play of *Titch* to give a performance for the class. Are they confident enough to give a school performance?

■   Ask the group that looked at the other books to share with the class what they found. Would they recommend the books to the other children? Can they tell you why? Leave the books on display while the familiar situations are still being explored.

■   Did the children find it useful and/or helpful to read books about children in different situations? Did they enjoy the books? How did they feel about the end of *Titch*? What have they learned about being in familiar but unwanted situations?

■   Do the others agree about the emotion faces selected to match the other books?

Lesson Two

Intended learning

■   To understand that personal titles and names begin with a capital letter.

■   To use a variety of texts to reinforce the concept.

With the whole class

■   Before the lesson, write on the board some names of staff members with their titles. For example, Mr Smith, Mrs Jones and Miss Kaur.

■   Can the children read the names? Point to the title of each name and read it with the children. Ask *"Are these the actual names of the teachers?"* Can they tell you what the titles are? Do they know what they mean? Explain that we use a title for people when they are not members of our families or our friends.

■   Tell the children that most people have Mrs, Miss, Ms or Mr as their title. Go through each of these with them and ask who would have each, ie which gender. Do they know the difference between each of the female titles? If not, explain. Can the children tell you all the titles of staff in the school?

■   Can the children tell you any other titles? Some examples are Dr, Sir, Professor, Lord and Captain. Make a list. Ask the children to try to find some others to add to the list later. Look at the titles offered and discuss the gender they apply to. For example, does 'Dr' always apply to a man? Does 'Sir'?

■   Ask the children what they notice about the way the titles are written. Point out that we always use a capital letter when writing titles. Ask *"What do you think your titles are at the moment?"* Write on the board 'Miss' and 'Master'. Explain that the latter is an old title, not used very much today, but can still be used for boys. Explain that 'Miss' is used both for girls and for ladies who are not married. Give a few examples of the children's names and their titles. For example, 'Miss Simret Bassra' and 'Master John Clayton'.

With the lower-achievers

With adult support

Choose from:

1   Ensure the children have understood that titles are written with a capital letter. Using the titles and names of staff members, and working closely with the children, ask them to make a list.

2   Using Resource sheet 12b, ask the children to rewrite the titles correctly. They should then complete the crossword puzzle. Give support if necessary.

3   Ask the children to tell you the titles and names of their family members. Ask each child to write these in a list. Can they add their doctor and dentist? Give help with family names where necessary.

Teacher-independent activities

Choose from:

1   Ask the children to draw a family portrait. Underneath the picture of each member they should write the title and family name. Remind them to use capital letters.

2   Give the children a selection of three or four familiar books. (Check beforehand that these contain examples of titles.) Ask them to look through these and write any titles and names that appear in the stories.

3   Prepare a sheet of A4 divided in half and headed 'Male' and 'Female' or appropriate equivalents. Ask the children to work in pairs and write in the correct section as many titles as they can think of and find. Remind them that these must have capital letters.

4   Ask the children to complete Resource sheet 12b by themselves.

Plenary session

■   Can the children tell you any new titles they discovered? Add these to the list already started in the whole-class session.

■   Ask *"What's the important thing to remember when writing people's titles?"* Do they understand they must use capital letters?

■   Is there anything they found difficult about the lesson?

Lesson Three

Intended learning

■   To focus on some high frequency words from the NLS framework that appear in *Titch*.

■   To follow the text and be able to read and use appropriately each high frequency word.

With the whole class

■   Write on the board the words 'had', 'that' and 'was'. Ask the children to read them.

■   Reread the text of *Titch* asking the children to supply the high frequency words.

■   Ask the children to give you some examples of each word used in a different sentence. Think of nursery rhymes that use these words, such as 'Mary had a little lamb'.

■   Ask the children to spell the words phonically with you pointing to each letter as they say it. If necessary, remind them that the consonant digraph 'th' should be sounded as a single phoneme. Ask some of them to come up and write the words on the board again by themselves.

With the lower-achievers

With adult support

Choose from:

1   Read *Titch* aloud with the children, encouraging them to supply the high frequency words.

2   Using Resource sheet 12c, ask the children to supply the appropriate high frequency word for each sentence. Give support where necessary.

3   Play 'Beat the Clock' where each child is encouraged to spell each high frequency word correctly within a given time. Give 20 to 25 seconds per word to start with and gradually reduce the allowed time. (These times are arbitrary and should be adjusted according to each child's ability.) Don't put the children into a panic about this. Praise them if they succeed.

4   Ask the children to write a sentence using each high frequency word. The adult should support and/or scribe where necessary.

Teacher-independent activities

Choose from:

1   Prepare a set of cards each with one letter from each high frequency word written on it. There should be a set of cards for each child (ie ten cards each). The children play a game where all the cards are put into a bag and the children take turns to select a card. They try to build up the high frequency words. If the card they choose cannot be used in that turn, it must be returned to the bag.

2   Use a 'Snakes and Ladders' board for a game where the children play in groups of three or four. When they reach the bottom of a snake or a ladder, they must spell one of the high frequency words named by another child. (That child can check with a flash card whether it was spelled correctly.) If they succeed, they can go up the snake or the ladder. If they fail they just wait for their next turn to move on. The winner reaches the top of the board first.

3   Prepare a sheet of A4 per child, divided into three, with a high frequency word in each box. Ask the children to do the writing themselves, if possible. Ask them to put one tick into the appropriate box each time they come across that word in the text of *Titch*.

Plenary session

■   A spokesperson from each group should share with the rest of the class what their group did.

■   Ask them to play a game of 'Hangman' without your support using the high frequency words. Act as arbiter/supervisor but encourage the children to do the writing, choosing and letter-guessing by themselves.

■   What did the children enjoy about the lesson? Was there anything they found difficult? Can they all recognise, read and spell each of the high frequency words that were explored?

Name _____

■ Draw Titch, Pete and Mary.

Titch	Pete	Mary

■ Complete the sentence using the words to help you.

Titch was sad because _____

_____

| small | bigger | things | Pete | Mary |

■ Who owns these things?

_____   _____   _____

Name _____

■ Write these titles with capital letters.

ms   mrs   mr   miss   dr   sir   lord   master

_____

■ Complete the crossword. All the answers are titles. Don't forget to write the capital letters.

Down

1. A lady who is not married is called _ _ _ _

2. Earl is sometimes called L _ _ _

3. A lady who is married is called _ _ _

5. A man is called _ _

· ·

Across

1. Sometimes a lady is called _ _

3. A little boy is called _ _ _ _ _ _

4. A person who looks after sick people is called _ _

6. A man teacher is sometimes called _ _ _

■ Do you know any more titles? Write them here.

_____   _____   _____

■ Choose the right word to finish each sentence.

| had | that | was |

1. Titch _____ a little boy.

2. Pete _____ a big drum to play with.

3. Titch planted a seed _____ grew into a big plant.

■ Write three sentences of your own using these words.

_____

_____

_____

Stories with fantasy settings

Overall aims

- To discuss the nature of fantasy stories.
- To add question marks to questions.
- To revise and consolidate the terms 'vowel' and 'consonant'.

Featured book

Where the Wild Things Are by Maurice Sendak

Story synopsis

Max is sent to bed without anything to eat because he has been naughty. His mother calls him a wild thing and sends him to his room. While there, his room becomes a fantasy land through which Max travels to the place where the wild things live. He is not afraid of them and he tames them with a magic trick. They make him king of the wild things. After some time of being wild with the wild things, Max smells good things to eat and returns home. There, in his now normal bedroom, is his supper on the table.

Lesson One

Intended learning

- To discuss the nature of fantasy stories.
- To work with the featured text and analyse the likelihood of the story being real.

With the whole class

- Introduce the story to the children. Show the cover (opened to display the full picture) and read the title. Ask what they think the story might be about. Read it to them. Show the pictures as the story is being read. Stop where appropriate and indicate features of the pictures which illustrate that part of the text.

- Ask the children whether they think this story is true. Can they give you reasons for their answers? Ask them to give a possible explanation for the events in the story. For example, was Max just having a dream? Is it a fantasy story in its own right? Or is the story

the result of Max's imagination while he is in his room alone?

- Explain that a story which is obviously untrue is called a 'fantasy' story. Can they tell you fantasy stories they have read themselves or somebody has read to them? List their suggestions.

- Explore with the children what features might be in a fantasy story. For example, imaginative creatures such as those in *Where the Wild Things Are*, fairies, goblins and the world of 'the little people'; activities or happenings that are obviously unreal, such as people flying (*Peter Pan*) or shrinking (*Alice's Adventures in Wonderland*); or animals speaking (*Paddington Bear* or *Winnie the Pooh*) or unlikely settings or places. Make a list of these features and leave it displayed for reference. Select a range of fantasy stories for a table display while the teaching point is being covered.

With the lower-achievers

With adult support

Choose from:

1   Read the story to the children again. Look at the pictures of Max's bedroom when the forest is growing. Point out the faint outlines of the furniture. Have they seen trees and plants like these anywhere? Do they think the story is real? Why?/Why not? Using the list of features of a fantasy story drawn up in the whole-class session, ask the children to say which features are in *Where the Wild Things Are*. Giving support where necessary, encourage the children to make a list of these on a sheet of paper headed 'Where the Wild Things Are'. Display this list alongside the main general list.

2   Using Resource sheet 13a, discuss which pictures represent real and which fantasy situations. Can they tell you how they decide which is real and which fantasy? Ask them to label each picture 'Real' or 'Fantasy'.

3   Ask the children to cut out different body parts from pictures in an old magazine and stick these onto a sheet of paper, to create a fantasy creature. Ask them to write a few words about their creature. What is its name?

Teacher-independent activities

Choose from:

1   Ask the children to choose another fantasy story they are able to read by themselves. They should draw the main character from the story and write the name. Challenge them to write a few words about the story.

2   Ask the children to complete Resource sheet 13a.

3   Using comics, ask the children to work in pairs and decide which stories are obviously fantasy and which are realistic. They should refer to the list of features drawn up in the whole-class session. Ask them to write a list of story titles under each category if possible.

Plenary session

■   Can the children tell you some of the features of a fantasy story? Cover the list beforehand and see how many features they remember. Together make up your own fantasy story.

■   Do they enjoy fantasy stories more than 'realistic' stories? Can they tell you why or why not?

Lesson Two

Intended learning

■   To explore the nature of questions and understand the term 'question mark'.

■   To add question marks to questions.

With the whole class

■   Tell the children you want them to listen carefully to the words you are going to say. Explain that they mustn't yet say anything back to you no matter what they hear! Then slowly ask a number of questions, pausing between them to allow the children to think. Some examples are *"Where are you going?"*, *"Why is the baby crying?"*, *"What did the boy eat for dinner?"*, *"Who scored the winning goal?"*, *"How do we make a cup of tea?"* and *"When do we have snow and ice?"*

Ask the children what type of sentences these were. Can they tell you that you asked several questions?

■   Ask *"What is a question?"* Explore with them that we ask questions when we want to know something or when we want to clarify something. Discuss what the 'question words' are: 'Who', 'What', 'Where', 'When', 'Why' and 'How'. Write these on the board, without questions marks at this point. Can the children give you some examples of instances when we need to ask questions? (The issue of word order in questions is looked at in Years 2 and 4, so at this stage don't address this point.) Leave the words on the board.

■   Draw a question mark on the board. Ask the children what it is. Can they tell you what it is used for? Talk about where we would use question marks. Explain that we use them when writing questions. Agree some questions and write them on the board. For example, 'How old are you?' and 'Do you like sweets?'

■   Ask some of the children to come and put a question mark after each question word written earlier on the board.

■   Ask for volunteers to write a question on the board to include the question mark. Give them a different colour to highlight the question mark.

With the lower-achievers

With adult support

Choose from:

1   Prepare for each child a sheet of A4 with 'What', 'When', 'Why', 'Where', 'Who' and 'How' (in that order) written down the left side. Read these with them and point out that most of them begin with 'wh'. Explain that 'who' sounds different from the other 'wh' words and has the same sound at the beginning as 'how'. Encourage them to write a question for each word. Give support where necessary.

2   Play a game of 'Question – True or False?' Ask each child in turn to answer 'True' or 'False' to your statement, which is either a question (using one of the question words) or a sentence. For example, *"Catherine, 'When is your birthday?'"* is

a question. *True or false?*" or *"Michael, 'I love to go swimming' is a question. True or false?"* Give a token or tiddlywink for each correct answer. The winner has the highest number of tokens at the end of the game.

3 Give out copies of Resource sheet 13b. Give support where necessary.

4 Together, look through *Where the Wild Things Are* for question marks. Ask the children to choose other favourite books and look through them for question marks. Read the questions together.

Teacher-independent activities

Choose from:

1 Ask the children to look at a nursery rhyme book and write some examples of questions with question marks. For example, they should discover 'Mary, Mary… how does your garden grow?', 'Where's the boy who looks after the sheep?', 'Baa, baa, black sheep have you any wool?' and so on.

2 Make some question word cards ('When?', 'Why?' and so on). The sets should be put inside bags. Give each pair of children a set. They take it in turns to take a card out of the bag and have to make up a question with that word. If their partner agrees it is a correct question the first child takes a counter. Can the partner answer the question? If so, they take a counter. They then change over. How many counters do they have at the end of the session?

3 Ask the children to work in pairs and refer to the list of question words written in the whole-class session. They should make up and write a question for each word. If they can't write some of the words they need for the question perhaps they could draw a picture instead. Explain that they will have the opportunity to show their questions in the plenary session.

4 Let the children complete Resource sheet 13b.

Plenary session

(Before coming together again, cover the list of question words.)

■ Ask different children to write one question word on the board. Read them together. Uncover the list and ask whether any words were forgotten.

■ Ask a volunteer to draw a giant question mark on the board. Ask the children what it means and what it is for.

■ Ask those children who worked independently to make up and write questions for the question words written in the whole-class session to show and read out their questions.

■ Ask if everybody understands why and where we use question marks.

Lesson Three

Intended learning

■ To revise and consolidate the terms 'vowel' and 'consonant'.

■ To identify vowels and consonants, while using the terms correctly.

With the whole class

(Ensure that the alphabet is displayed in the classroom before beginning this lesson.)

■ Write the word 'vowel' on the board and read it with the children. Can they tell you what it means? Remind them of the work they did in the Reception year on vowels. Can they tell you what the vowels are? Write them on the board. Ask for words with the vowels at the beginning or in the middle. Can the children write these on the board themselves? (Challenge them to think of words with a vowel at the end. For example, 'pizza', 'Santa', 'disco' and 'pasta'.)

■ Write the word 'consonant' on the board and read it with the children. Again, remind them that they met this word in the Reception year. Can they tell you what it means? Can they give you some examples? Choose a consonant such as 'g' and ask the children to think of some words that begin with it. Write some of them on the board. Now ask if they can think of any words ending with 'g'. Write these words up.

■ Using the alphabet display, play a game of 'Which Vowel? Which Consonant?' Name a child and ask them for a specified vowel or consonant. For example, *"Hisham, which is the third vowel?"* or *"Samantha, which is the seventh consonant?"* (Warn them that they mustn't count the number of letters from the beginning of the alphabet to find the answer, but the vowels or consonants.)

With the lower-achievers

With adult support

Choose from:

1   Ensure the children fully understand the terms 'vowel' and 'consonant'. If more practice is needed, play games using alphabet flash cards. For example, where the children have to sort the mixed cards into vowels and consonants as quickly as possible, or where they have to identify the card being held up as a vowel or consonant, as quickly as possible. They could keep a record of their times and try to beat their own record. Ensure the game is fun, however, without pressure or panic.

2   Give the children copies of Resource sheet 13c. For the last part of the sheet they can write just 'c' and 'v'.

3   Look at the first page of *Where the Wild Things Are* and ask the children to find either vowels or consonants. Then ask them to find on the page a specific word and write it. For example, *"Can you find a word with the medial vowel 'a'?"* ('Max')

Teacher-independent activities

Choose from:

1   Ask the children to complete Resource sheet 13c. They could then try to write a sentence for one of the given words on the back of the sheet.

2   Prepare a tape with c-v-c words recorded onto it. Give the children a tray of plastic letters and ask them to sort these into vowels and consonants. They should then listen to the tape and make each of the c-v-c words, selecting the correct letters from the vowel and consonant piles. Keep these on display while doing this work.

3   Give the children a large sheet of paper divided in two, lengthways. Ask them to write 'Vowels' on one half and on the other 'Consonants' and then write the letters of the alphabet into the correct sections. Ask them to use as many different colours as possible.

Plenary session

■ A child from each group should share with the other children what their group did. Ensure they use the terms 'vowel' and 'consonant' while they explain their activities.

■ Ask the group that worked independently to make the large vowel and consonant chart, to come to the front of the class and show the others what they did. Put the chart on the wall for display while continuing with this work.

■ Does everybody fully understand what a vowel is? Do they all know what a consonant is? Was there anything about the lesson that they found difficult? What did they find easy?

■ Look at the pictures.
  Write **Real** or **Fantasy** under each one.

_____

_____

_____

_____

■ Use the question words to complete the questions. Then write in the question marks.

When	Why	What	Where	Who	How

_____ is your birthday

_____ do you live

_____ was Max sent to his room

_____ brings our Christmas presents

_____ do dogs like to eat

_____ do you come to school

■ Choose three of the words and write your own questions.

_____

_____

_____

■ Write the vowels in these boxes.

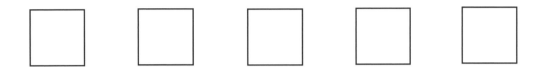

■ Write some consonants in these boxes.

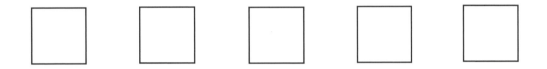

■ Complete the words under the pictures with a vowel or a consonant.

_en   _og   _gg   _pple   _at

■ Read the words and label the letters.

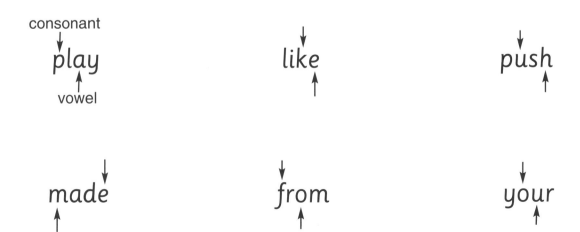

consonant
↓
play
↑
vowel

↓
like
↑

↓
push
↑

↓
made
↑

↓
from
↑

↓
your
↑

Poems with themes

Overall aims

- To study several poems on a common theme.
- To relate the theme to own life/experiences.
- To use poetry as a stimulus for further work.

Featured book

Bags of Poems: Family Album collected by Jill Bennett

Lesson One

Chosen poems

'My grannies' by June Crebbin and 'Grandpa never sleeps' by Mark Burgess (See page 105)

Intended learning

- To work with several poems about the family and to identify this theme.
- To relate the theme and the poems to own life/experiences.
- To use the theme as the basis for further work.

With the whole class

- Enlarge copies of 'My grannies' by June Crebbin and 'Grandpa never sleeps' by Mark Burgess.

- Ask the children to talk about their families. (Be conscious of different cultures/backgrounds in the class and treat these with sensitivity.) Ask the children to name relations – mum, brother, aunty and so on. Write these words on the board. When grandparents are mentioned write the relevant words such as 'Nanna', 'Grandpa', 'Pops', 'Gran' and put a circle around each one.

- Tell the children they are going to read some poems about families in the next couple of lessons. Today they're going to explore some poems about grandparents.

- Read 'My grannies' with the children, pointing to the text during reading. Ask them whether any of their grannies do these things. What does their granny do that irritates them? What does she do that they like?

- Read 'Grandpa never sleeps' with the children, pointing to the text during reading. Can they tell you what the child in the poem thinks about the grandpa? Do their grandfathers ever do things like the grandpa in the poem? Ask them to talk about some of their grandpas' activities.

With the lower-achievers

With adult support

Choose from:

1. Make a book of 'Things We Do with Granny/Grandpa'. Ask the children to write about or draw pictures of their favourite activities with their grandparents/older relations. Give support where necessary.

2. Ask the children for words which describe their granny/ grandpa. Divide these into physical descriptions and characteristics. Make a word wall with them. Add to this as new words are learned.

3. Using Resource sheet 14a ask the children to draw a picture of their granny/grandpa. If they don't have one they could draw either another older family member or a granny/grandpa they would like to have. Then, using the word wall, they should write words which describe the granny/grandpa. Give support where necessary.

4. Ask the children to draw a family tree of their immediate family and grandparents. They will need help with setting this out. (Or use Generic sheet 12, page 128.)

Teacher-independent activities

Choose from:

1. Ask the children to make 'grandparents cards' for the 'Happy Families' set. Play the game with the new cards added.

2. Make copies of the family tree diagram on Generic sheet 12 (page 128). Ask the children to draw their own family tree. If they don't

have any of these family members tell them this is a tree of the family they would like to have. Or they could do a tree of someone else's family, fictional or real.

3 Prior to this activity prepare a sheet of A4 per child, divided in half. Write 'Granny is...' and 'Grandpa is...' in the sections. Ask the children to choose words from the word wall that describe the grandparents and write these in the correct section. Can they write one or two sentences about their grandparents/older relatives?

Plenary session

■ Ask the children to choose their favourite poem of the two and read it again, encouraging everyone to join in.

■ Challenge the children to find some other poems about either grandparents or other family members, perhaps from home or the local library. Ask them to bring these into school to share with the class.

■ Ask the other groups to report back on what their activities were about. Tell the children that next time, they'll explore some poems about different family members.

Lesson Two

Chosen poems

'Friends again' by Paul Rogers and 'My little sister' by Ann Bonner (See page 106)

Intended learning

■ To read more poems on the family theme.

■ To use the poems as stimulus for writing own poems.

With the whole class

■ Enlarge copies of 'My little sister' and 'Friends again'.

■ Remind the children of the poems they read about grandparents. Tell them that today they are going to look at some poems about brothers and sisters.

■ Ask the children to tell the class about their brothers and sisters. Ask what they like/dislike about their brothers or sisters. If anyone doesn't have a brother or sister ask them if they would like one and if so what they would want them to be like.

■ Read 'My little sister' with the children, pointing to the text during reading. Ask the children who have younger siblings if they feel the same way as the child in the poem. Use the word 'sibling' and explain what it means, showing them that they can find out by referring to a dictionary.

■ Read 'Friends again' with the children and ask them to point to the text during reading. Ask the children who else this poem could be about as well as siblings. Talk about the notion of falling out with or being annoyed by brothers and sisters. Discuss how they make friends again.

With the lower-achievers

With adult support

Choose from:

1 Work closely with the children to write a poem about their sibling or an imaginary one. Tell them the poem doesn't have to rhyme. Let them refer to the chosen poems for ideas if they wish. (The poem need not be longer than three or four lines.) Ask them to write their poem on Resource sheet 14c, using the words on it to help them if they wish.

2 Using Resource sheet 14b, ask the children to read the words that might describe their brother/sister. Give help where necessary. They should draw a picture of a sibling in the centre and then join the relevant describing words to the picture. If possible they should then write a sentence about the sibling or just write their name.

3 Read the two poems with the children again. Ask them to say what they liked about these

and why. Ask them whether they think the poems are realistic and why/why not.

4   Make a chart showing the group's brothers and sisters. Ask them to write on it the names of their siblings. Let those who don't have any add a brother and/or sister they would like. Put a list next to it showing the tally of younger/ older brothers/sisters.

Teacher-independent activities

Choose from:

1   Give the children pieces of paper the size of playing cards. Ask them to draw pictures of their siblings, one to each card. They should write the name of the sibling at the bottom of the picture. Using the 'Happy Families' cards, ask the children to sort out all the siblings and put them together with their own sibling cards. Make a display of these.

2   Using Resource sheet 14c, ask the children to write a poem about themselves and their brother or sister. Tell them that it doesn't have to rhyme and they may use the words on the sheet to help them if they wish.

3   Ask the children to make a list of the brothers and sisters of all the children in the class. They could make a bar-graph of siblings writing the axes and data themselves.

Plenary session

■   Ask the children who wrote their own poems to read these to the class. After the lesson either display the poems or make a class book for the class to read during unstructured times.

■   Ask the children which their favourite poem is of all those explored. Can they tell you why they like it? Are there any of the chosen poems they did not like? Can they tell you why?

■   Challenge the children to suggest other themes that might be good for poetry. Some ideas could include food, monsters, school or weather.

My grannies

I hate it, in the holiday,
When Grandma brings her pets to stay –
Her goat, her pig, her seven rats
Scare our dog and chase our cats.
Her budgies bite, her parrots shout –
And guess who has to clean them out?

My other Gran, the one I like,
Always brings her motor-bike,
And when she takes me for a ride
To picnic in the countryside,
We zoom up hills and whizz round bends –
I hate it when her visit ends!

by June Crebbin

Grandpa never sleeps

Grandpa doesn't sleep at night,
He never sleeps a wink.
Instead he tinkers with the car
Or mends the kitchen sink.

Sometimes he picks the rhubarb
Or polishes the floor.
And other nights he's shopping
At the local all-night store.

Last night he papered half the hall
And built a garden shed.
But when the rest of us got up
He didn't go to bed.

I don't know how he does it,
He's always on the go.
Grandpa never sleeps AT ALL –
At least, I think that's so...

by Mark Burgess

My little sister

My sister and I always fight.
I'm sure she's wrong. I think I'm right.

She pinches my toys when I'm not there.
She cheats at games. She's never fair.

She leaves her clothes all over the place
If I complain she pulls a face.

Every morning I have to wait
To take her to school... we're always late...

But however naughty she can be
Nothing must hurt her. She's smaller than me.

by Ann Bonner

Friends again

My brother bashed me with a stick.
I hit him with the hose.
He pulled my hair. I scratched his face.
He thumped me on the nose.

I bit his leg; he screamed. I screamed.
We called each other names.
Then Mum came out and asked us why
We couldn't play nice games.

I sulked. He moped. I frowned. He smiled.
I let him in my den.
He offered me a sticky sweet,
And now we're friends again.

by Paul Rogers

■ Draw a picture of a granny or grandad.

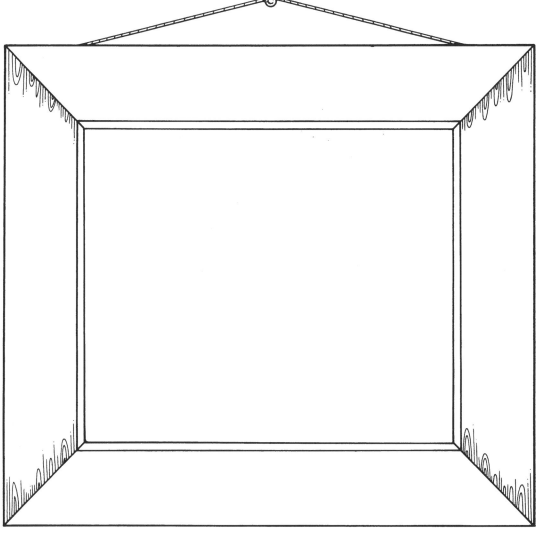

■ Write some words about a granny and grandad.
Use the word wall to help you.

_____   _____

_____   _____

_____   _____

_____   _____

■ Read the words. Draw a picture of your brother or sister.

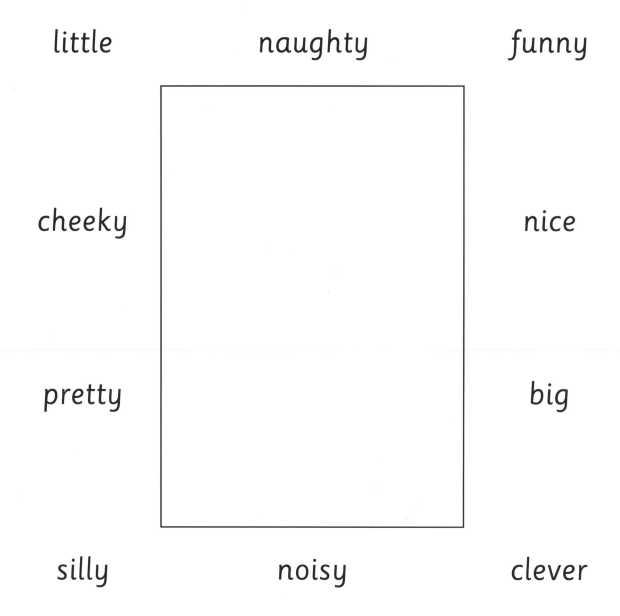

little   naughty   funny

cheeky   nice

pretty   big

silly   noisy   clever

■ Circle the words that remind you of your brother or sister.

■ Write about your brother or sister.

_____

Name _____

■ Write a poem about your brother or sister.
   Use the words to help you.

 brother

 sister

My _____

My _____ is _____

 sweet

We sometimes _____

 fight

And always _____

 play

Mum says we _____

 scruffy

But I say we _____

■ Draw your brother or sister here.

 happy

 cross

 love

 smile

friends   naughty

Poems for writing poetry

Overall aims

- To revisit several traditional poems and rhymes and explore them in more depth.
- To use the poems studied as models for own work by substituting words.
- To use the poems studied as models for own work by elaborating on the text.

Lesson One

Chosen rhymes

'Yankee Doodle' and 'Hey diddle, diddle' (See page 113)

Intended learning

- To revisit several traditional poems and rhymes and explore them in more depth.
- To use the poems studied as models for own work by substituting words.

With the whole class

- Enlarge the copy of 'Yankee Doodle' and 'Hey diddle, diddle'. Tell the children they are going to explore some nursery rhymes.
- Read 'Yankee Doodle' encouraging the children to join in. Point to the text during reading. Ask if they know where Yankee Doodle came from. Ask them if they think the rhyme is silly or funny. Ask for reasons for their answers.
- Tell the children that they are going to make up their own rhyme about Yankee Doodle. Using sticky notes, blank off the words 'pony', 'feather' and 'macaroni'. Ask for suggestions to replace those words that have been covered. Explain that the suggestions can be anything. For example, 'pony' could be replaced by 'bicycle', 'donkey', 'skateboard', 'scooter' and so on; 'feather' could be replaced by 'flag', 'carrot', 'light bulb' and so on. Write the new words on the sticky notes. Point to the text during reading.

- Using the enlarged copy of 'Hey diddle, diddle', read it to the children encouraging them to join in.
- Ask them if they think the rhyme is silly or funny. Ask for reasons for their answers. Explain that this is known as a nonsense rhyme. Ask them why they think this is. Discuss what a nonsense rhyme is.

With the lower-achievers

With adult support

Choose from:

1   Using the enlarged copy of 'Hey diddle, diddle' blank off with sticky notes the words 'moon', 'dish' and 'spoon'. Read the rhyme with the children, encouraging them to suggest alternatives for the covered words. Explain that the words can be almost anything since this is a nonsense rhyme. Say that the words do not have to rhyme. Write the agreed suggestions on the sticky notes.

2   Using Resource sheet 15a, ask the children to write new words into the spaces of 'Hey diddle, diddle'. (If they have done activity 1, encourage them to choose their own words and not to copy from the enlarged version.) Tell them that the words can be almost anything since this is a nonsense rhyme. Explain that the words do not have to rhyme. Ask them to illustrate their new poem.

3   Encourage the children to learn the new version of 'Yankee Doodle' made up during the whole-class session. Allocate a line to each child to learn and practise by saying it aloud. When they are confident, ask them to say their lines so that they recite the whole poem. Ask them to give a class performance.

4   Using Resource sheet 15b, and giving reading support where necessary, ask the children to substitute the missing words of 'Jack and Jill' from the given selection. They should then illustrate their sheets.

Teacher-independent activities

Choose from:

1 Ask the children to draw a large picture of Yankee Doodle from the original rhyme, and another from the new version. Ask them to write the rhyme for each picture on the bottom, highlighting in a different colour the words which were changed. Make a display gallery of 'Yankee Doodle Before and After'.

2 Let the children complete resource sheet 15a, making up a new version of 'Hey diddle, diddle' and illustrating it.

3 Using Resource sheet 15b, ask the children to substitute the missing words of 'Jack and Jill' from the given selection. They should then illustrate their sheets.

Plenary session

- Ask somebody from each group to share with the rest of the class what they did. Ask them to show the other children their sheets, books or pictures if appropriate.

- Can they tell you what a nonsense rhyme is? Do they enjoy working with nonsense rhymes? Can they tell you why? Do they think nonsense rhymes are silly, boring or good fun?

- Ask the group who learned the new version of 'Yankee Doodle' to give a class performance.

Lesson Two

Chosen poems

'Doctor Foster' and 'Hickory, dickory, dock' (See page 113)

Intended learning

- To revisit several traditional poems and rhymes and explore them in more depth.

- To use the poems studied as models for own work by elaborating on the text.

With the whole class

- Enlarge two copies of 'Doctor Foster' and 'Hickory, dickory, dock'.

- Read 'Doctor Foster' with the children, encouraging them to join in. Point to the text during reading. Ask them for suggestions for other places that Doctor Foster might have visited. Write several suggestions on the board. Explain that the places do not have to be town names but could also be venues, for example jogging in the park.

- Ask the children for suggestions for the weather conditions in the next part of Doctor Foster's adventures. Then ask them what happened to Doctor Foster in the new place. Tell them that they should try to connect the event with the weather. For example, if it was snowing, Doctor Foster's toes froze.

- Write the new words on sticky notes and put these over the original words on one of the enlarged copies. Hang the two copies side by side on the wall and display them.

With the lower-achievers

With adult support

Choose from:

1 Using the enlarged copy of 'Hickory, dickory, dock', read it with the children, encouraging them to join in. Point to the text during reading. Tell them that they are going to write the next part of the rhyme. Say the rhyme together again but substitute 'the clock struck two' and encourage the children to say what happened next. For example, 'the clock struck two, the mouse found a shoe' or 'the clock struck three, the mouse went for tea' and so on. Continue this with upward counting according to the ability of the children. Giving support, ask them to write the new poem on a large sheet of paper. Challenge them to learn it for a class performance.

2 Give the children copies of Resource sheet 15c. They may use the words around the sheet or their own. Give support where necessary.

3 Look through other anthologies and ask the children to choose a favourite nursery rhyme.

Recite it together pausing at different places, encouraging the children to substitute alternative words. For example, 'Sing a song of ___, A pocketful of ___, Four and twenty ___, ___ in a ___, When the ___ was ___, The ___ began to ___, Wasn't that a ___ to set before a ___!' Giving support, challenge the children to write the new version.

Teacher-independent activities

Choose from:

1   Give each child a sheet of A4 paper divided in half lengthways. Ask them to look at the two enlarged copies of 'Doctor Foster' (the original and the new one made up during the whole-class session). They should put the original words in one column and more new ones of their own in the other.

2   Let the children complete Resource sheet 15c. They may use the words around the sheet or their own.

3   Ask the children to work in pairs and choose another nursery rhyme. They should make a new one by substituting words. Tell them they need to change only two or three words. Ask them to write and illustrate their new rhyme. Challenge them to learn it for a class performance.

Plenary session

■   Ask the children who learned a new version of 'Hickory, dickory, dock' to give a class performance. Ask if any of the other children would like to recite their new version nursery rhymes.

■   Ask each group to report back to the class on what activities they did. Encourage them to show sheets or illustrations to the other children and explain what they did. Make a display of their work.

Yankee Doodle

Yankee Doodle came to town,

Riding on a pony;

He stuck a feather in his cap

And called it macaroni.

Hey diddle, diddle

Hey diddle, diddle,

The cat and the fiddle,

The cow jumped over the moon;

The little dog laughed

To see such fun,

And the dish ran away with the spoon.

Doctor Foster

Doctor Foster went to Gloucester

In a shower of rain.

He stepped in a puddle right up to his middle

And never went there again.

Hickory, dickory, dock

Hickory, dickory, dock,

The mouse ran up the clock.

The clock struck one, the mouse ran down,

Hickory, dickory, dock.

■ Put new words into the nursery rhyme.

Hey diddle, diddle,

The cat and the fiddle,

The cow jumped over the _____

The little dog laughed

To see such fun,

And the _____ ran away

With the _____

■ Draw a picture of the new rhyme.

■ Choose the words to make a new nursery rhyme.

Jack and Jill went up the hill

To fetch a _____

■ pot of paint   ■ baby's nappy

Jack fell down and broke his crown

And Jill felt very _____

■ faint   ■ happy

■ Draw a picture about your new rhyme.

■ Write some more verses of 'Hickory, dickory,
  dock'. You can use the words to help you.

screw    shoe

Hickory, dickory, dock,
The mouse ran up the clock,
The clock struck two,    found
ate The mouse _____
tea Hickory, dickory, dock.

 flea

Hickory, dickory, dock,
The mouse ran up the clock,
drank The clock struck three,
The mouse _____
door Hickory, dickory, dock.

Hickory, dickory, dock,
shut The mouse ran up the clock,
The clock struck four,
The mouse _____
began
Hickory, dickory, dock.

 snore    had

said

she

and

was

apple	bin	car	dog
egg	flower	gate	hat
insect	jug	kite	leg
man	nail	octopus	peg
queen	rabbit	star	tap
umbrella	violin	window	x-ray
yacht	zebra		

the	want
and	play
I	with
can	come
like	.	my
to	.	me

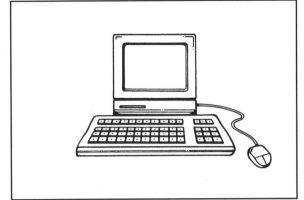 

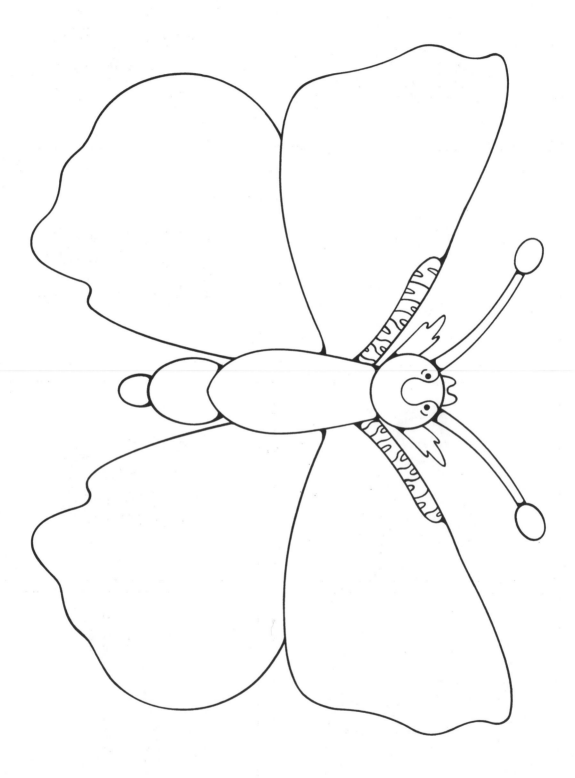

bl	br	cr
ch	cl	fl
fr	gl	gr
pl	pr	sh
sk	sm	sp
st	th	tr

Family tree

_____